More Praise for *Selling Results!*

"Bill Stinnett's sales philosophy is based on helping your customers create value by achieving their business goals. This book will teach you how to sell outcomes and results instead of products and services."

David Booth
Senior Vice President and US Country Manager, Technology Solutions Group
Hewlett-Packard Company

"Stinnett's tools and techniques for opportunity management are among the most highly evolved and pragmatic I have seen. The concepts and materials presented in *Selling Results!* should be adopted by any sales organization that is serious about improving the predictability of their sales results."

George Fischer
Senior Vice President and General Manager, Americas' Sales
CA, Inc. (Computer Associates)

"*Selling Results!* is a great resource for advising and teaching any sales professional how to manage their way through the ever more complicated sales process."

Adam J. Klaber
Global CRM Leader
IBM Global Business Services

"What impresses me most about *Selling Results!* is that Stinnett cuts directly to the specific steps salespeople need to take to be more successful. These are the distilled best practices of the selling profession."

Don Grantham
Executive Vice President, Global Sales and Services
Sun Microsystems, Inc.

"Stinnett hits a grand slam! Reading this book is an investment that will pay you back for years to come."

Colby Ward
Sales Director, Security and Access Management
Novell, Inc.

"Bill Stinnett provides the tools and infrastructure for maximizing sales, including a useful way to measure and manage the metrics that drive results."

Steven Mitchell
Radiology Consulting Leader
GE Healthcare

"The sales process is a road down which you and your customer travel together. *Selling Results!* paves the road, helps you avoid all the potholes and detours, and enables you to get to your destination faster than ever."

Gerhard Gschwandtner
Publisher
Selling Power Magazine

"No one should buy this book unless they want to radically change the way they think about selling. Stinnett offers a compete system for growing your sales by helping your customers achieve their business goals."

H. David Hennessey, Ph. D.
Professor of Marketing
Babson College

"*Selling Results!* is a wonderful extension of Bill Stinnett's unique approach to selling. A complete blueprint for maximizing your sales results."

Mohanbir Sawhney
McCormick Tribune Professor of Technology, Kellogg School of Management
Northwestern University

"This book presents a thoughtful and methodical approach to selling that is based on a thorough analysis of your customer's needs and expectations. It also provides the tools to put this methodology to use."

Vithala R. Rao
Deane W. Malott Professor of Management, Johnson Graduate School of Management
Cornell University

"This is a book for any serious salesperson. It introduces and combines many of the latest ideas in sales and presents them in a manner that makes sense."

Dan C. Weilbaker, Ph. D.
McKesson Pharmaceutical Group Professor of Sales
Northern Illinois University

"*Selling Results!* starts sales professionals on the journey of viewing their customers as partners rather than quick wins—a healthy basis for long-term relationships and increased revenue."

Carol Pillinger
Director of Education
Institute of Sales & Marketing Management (UK)

Selling Results!

The Innovative System for Maximizing Sales
by Helping Your Customers Achieve Their Business Goals

BILL STINNETT

McGraw-Hill

New York Chicago San Francisco Lisbon London
Madrid Mexico City Milan New Delhi San Juan
Seoul Singapore Sydney Toronto

1 2 3 4 5 6 7 8 9 0   FGR/FGR   0 9 8 7 6

ISBN-13: 978-0-07-147787-1
ISBN-10: 0-07-147787-X

This publication is designed to provide accurate and authoritative information in regard to the subject matter covered. It is sold with the understanding that the publisher is not engaged in rendering legal, accounting, or other professional service. If legal advice or other expert assistance is required, the services of a competent professional person should be sought.
— From a Declaration of Principles Jointly Adopted by a Committee of the American Bar Association and a Committee of Publishers and Associations

McGraw-Hill books are available at special discounts to use as premiums and sales promotions, or for use in corporate training programs. For more information, please write to the Director of Special Sales, Professional Publishing, McGraw-Hill, Two Penn Plaza, New York, NY 10121-2298. Or contact your local bookstore.

This book is printed on acid-free paper.

For Terri

Acknowledgments

The challenge with acknowledgments is not in determining who to include, but in deciding who *not* to include. I owe so much to so many. Of course, I must start with my immediate family. To my parents Bill and Erma Stinnett, who taught me character, integrity, and a tireless work ethic by firsthand example. To my brothers Gerald (Jerry) and Jim, and my sisters Glenda and Gloria; I appreciate your support, your encouragement, and your life-long belief in me.

I want to thank my former sales managers and mentors who have helped me in so many ways: Larry Smith, Herb Anderson, Sandy Elam, Ed Krolick, Michael Copperwhite, Marv Kaufman, Henry Quintin, Jeff Eaton, Shawn Hardy, Dave McKenna, Mark Smith, Mark Rossini, Jim White, Doug Brooke, and John Iuliano.

I believe I owe a debt of gratitude to those who have laid the foundation of sales doctrine upon which the material in this book was built. These include Dale Carnegie, Frank Bettger, Zig Ziglar, David Sandler, Tom Hopkins, Mack Hanan, Neil Rackham, Robert Miller and Stephen Heiman, Jim Holden, Michael Bosworth, Tony Parinello, Brian Tracy, Jeffrey Gitomer, Rick Page, and many others.

There are also a number of very special clients who have played a role in the evolution, field testing, and worldwide distribution of this material. This includes, but is not limited to, Mike Harrington, Mark Groudas, Dr. Richard Brooks, Tracey Tibedo, Scott Fulwider, Ken Jenson, Eric Bichet, Peter Lindstrom, Steve Miller, Bob Preves, Rick Laporte, Bob Hynes, Tony Bulleid, Mike Gengler, Mike Grendele,

Ed Raad, Paris Loesch, Terrie Stickel, Jim Spring, Sanjay Pingle, and Rick Abbate. I thank Scott Hurlbut for suggesting the title of this book and Jim Stillinger for introducing me to the fictional character "Clem."

Thank you to my editor, Donya Dickerson, as well as Seth Morris, Scott Kurtz, Peter McCurdy, Herb Schaffner, Philip Ruppel, Keith Fox, and the entire team at McGraw-Hill. Our work together has become a true partnership, and I sincerely appreciate all of you. I also want to take this opportunity to thank two very close friends, Jeff Bernier and Tim Schmidt, who have been a constant source of encouragement and inspiration to me for many years.

I sincerely thank the dedicated team at Sales Excellence, Inc. To Avanya Manasseh, working with you is a daily reminder of everything that is right and good about this world. I appreciate you more than you will ever know. To Dave Rohlf, I've enjoyed our friendship and admired your kind and gentle nature for so many years. As I aspire to be a better man, I hope to become more like you.

Finally, to Terri Johnson, you started out as my accountant, promoted yourself to editorial advisor, then chief collaborator, and have since become the love of my life. This book and every other aspect of my world is immeasureably better because of you. May our time together be just the beginning of a lifetime filled with hope, joy, and happiness.

Contents

Preface

Since the release of my first book, *Think Like Your Customer* (TLYC), I have been delightfully overwhelmed by the positive response I have received from sales and marketing professionals all over the world. That book has served as an effective training aid for the participants in the sales workshops offered by my company, Sales Excellence, Inc. It has also been a mechanism to introduce our concepts and materials to thousands of people who will never have the opportunity to attend one of our seminars.

As I began to envision the shape and scope of my second book, I sought to accomplish four specific objectives:

1. To extend the discussion around the practical application of the core concepts and principles introduced in *TLYC*, using the most current visual aids and practical examples.
2. To expand the subject matter to include several important skill sets that we teach in our seminars but were not addressed in *TLYC*, such as sales activity planning, sales prospecting (business development), opportunity management, presentation skills, and the principles of effective negotiation.
3. To publish and distribute the complete set of sales tools, templates, worksheets, and models that support the learning and utilization of all the skills we teach in our workshops.
4. To offer a blueprint for implementing all these tools, templates, worksheets and models in your sales environment.

The end product, *Selling Results!,* encompasses our complete sales methodology, which I call the Results-Based Selling Method.

This new book is written to stand on its own, but also to act as a natural extension of *TLYC.* If you have already read *TLYC,* then you will recognize many of the foundational principles revisted. But for those who haven't, I review the most important concepts and approaches within this book so you can make the most of this material.

As you read, you will encounter a broad array of tools, templates, and worksheets that can be used in planning your sales activities, managing opportunities, or simply developing your own knowledge base and skill set. All of these tools are available in electronic format. Please visit www.salesexcellence.com for more information.

I hope you enjoy reading this book and more importantly that you profit from it! I also hope you will use what you learn to help your customers profit from it too!

Bill Stinnett
Evergreen, Colorado
November 2006

CHAPTER ONE

Measuring, Managing, and Maximizing Your Sales Results

Pardon me for asking...but why are you reading this book? Perhaps a friend, a colleague, or your manager recommended it to you. Maybe you discovered it while browsing your local bookstore or your favorite bookseller's Web site. I'm not as concerned with how you acquired it, or how you have come to be reading the first page, as much as I am with why you would invest the time and effort to read this book and learn to use the ideas presented here. More simply put, what do you hope to get out of it?

This book, and everything in it, is designed to help you maximize your *selling results!* Those who are looking for a few new ideas will find them in short order. Those who decide to read a chapter or two will learn a number of foundational principles and ready-to-use techniques that they can weave into their personal selling style. But those who are interested in maximizing their own potential will devour this book—as they have doubtlessly devoured many others—taking the time to reflect on each chapter, highlight certain passages, and jot down ideas about how they can use this material in their own selling environment.

It might surprise you to learn that however you choose to use this book is fine with me. Like every other endeavor in life, the value you derive from this content will be directly proportional to the effort you put into applying it. But let's face it, reading this book is not the goal. The reason for reading this book is to acquire some new ideas, concepts, strategies, or techniques that will help you improve your sales results.

As you begin, take a minute to ask yourself, "Why would I do this? Why would I invest my precious time—which I could just as easily spend on my favorite hobby—in learning and applying the ideas in this book? What would I expect as a fair return on my investment of time and energy? What sort of measurable outcomes or results would I really like to achieve?"

By answering these questions, you will be far ahead of most of the people in your profession. When you answer the question "Why?" everything changes. Suddenly, *what* to do becomes much more obvious. Your creative mind gets involved, and you start to discover new ideas about *how* to do what you want to do everywhere you turn.

If you can clearly define what you want to accomplish—such as reducing your average pricing discount from 22 percent to 15 percent or shortening the length of your average sales cycle from 132 days to 120 days—you will find this book filled to the brim with ideas that can help you achieve those results. Before you finish this first chapter, you'll have a much better idea of which aspects of your sales game could use some improvement as well as what you'll need to do to take yourself—or your team—to the next level.

The Results-Based Selling Method

The sales methodology presented here is called the results-based selling method. It incorporates the most powerful and time-tested truths of selling into an easy-to-use set of strategies, tools, and techniques that can be implemented as a complete system or individually integrated with whatever tools and infrastructure you already use.

This philosophy of selling is based on two strongly held beliefs:

1. The best way to ensure that you achieve *your* desired sales results is to focus on helping your customers achieve *their* desired business results.
2. Sales professionals and their managers must plan, measure, and manage sales activity and behavior in order to maximize their sales results.

The results-based selling method is extremely customer-focused. As you will see, this approach is centered on better understanding your customer's business and how the products and services you sell can help them to achieve the results they already want to achieve. But this system is also focused on measuring, managing, and maximizing your own sales results. Because unless you make a fair profit and manage your own success, you may not be around to help your customers for very long.

This book provides an overview of the results-based selling methodology. In this chapter, we explore the world of selling and how some of the archaic concepts and approaches of the past keep salespeople from reaching their full potential. We discuss how the way we measure success drives our activity and how a new paradigm for planning, measuring, and managing sales behavior can revolutionize our sales results.

In Chapter Two we lay the foundation for building strong partner-based relationships with our customers that are based on helping them achieve their desired business results. In Chapters Three through Nine we delve into the essential skill sets required to be successful in the selling profession, including prospecting, qualification, presentation, and negotiation skills. Then, in the last chapter, we discuss how to implement this method in your sales environment as well as how to manage a results-based sales team.

The Ever-Changing World of Sales

A career in sales is often marked by constant change. There seems to be a never-ending stream of new technologies—such as wireless e-mail devices and Web-conferencing software—that promise to help us accomplish more work in less time. But for every new gadget that comes along to make our job easier, some other change makes our life that much more challenging.

As soon as you get comfortable with your territory, your company reorganizes the sales team by vertical markets as opposed to geography. Once you finally learn your company's product line, they get acquired by some other company, and you are immediately transferred to an entirely different group. Or maybe your company is one of the many that has decided to cut costs by eliminating all administrative help in the sales department. It never ends!

I still remember arriving at the office to begin my second full year in sales and being presented with my new "plan." My quota was just about double what it had been the year before. Commission rates were cut by an average of 25 percent. And—oh, by the way—we brought on several new sales reps, so my territory was literally cut in half. Surely this has never happened to you. Has it? Unfortunately, this kind of radical change has become the norm in many industries.

What I didn't understand back then was that executives have to manage their businesses to achieve certain objectives or risk losing their jobs. They have to cut costs in every way imaginable *and* produce consistent and predictable double-digit revenue growth. This kind of change is very difficult to manage, but managers and executives don't have a choice in the matter. Business owners and corporate share-holders demand results!

These expectations translate into a yearly demand for a minimum 10 percent increase in sales revenue from each salesperson—and usually much more than that! In order to survive and thrive in what I call the world of double-digit growth, we don't have the option of posting the same sales revenue as the year before. We have to improve our sales results by at least 10 or 20 percent every single year.

Your quota, your commission plan, and your territory are going to change. In fact, it's safe to assume that it's going to be harder to make your numbers every year. But if you or I approach each new year in the same way we approached the last, we are teetering on the edge of insanity by doing the same things over and over again and expecting different results.

Evolving as a Sales Professional

For several years, my only method for putting up bigger numbers was to work harder and longer. I adopted the "do more" approach to sales improvement: Send more letters, make more phone calls, and hold more meetings. But I found that it's not practical to just keep throwing more time at the job year after year. As the expectations on me continued to escalate, I eventually hit a threshold where doing more became almost impossible. Perhaps you've experienced this yourself.

We don't have the luxury of selling the same way we sold five years ago—or even two years ago—and simply doing more of the same. We can't focus solely on increasing sales activity as our only recipe for success. Activity is critical, and many of us probably do need to do more of one thing or another. But we also need to work on achieving better results from the time and effort we are already investing. We must continually evolve and rethink how we sell so that we are not just selling *more,* but selling *better* every single year.

If we subscribe only to the "do more" philosophy, then the quantity of the things we do becomes our primary focus. This whole line of thinking has been fueled by the old-fashioned premise that sales is a numbers game. But is that really all that sales is?

A numbers game, such as a slot machine, is strictly a game of chance. You put your quarter in, pull the handle, and something either happens or doesn't happen. You have no input, no influence on the outcome, and ultimately no control whatsoever. That's not what selling is. Is it?

Actually, selling is more like poker. There is a certain element of chance to poker. You can't control which cards you are dealt. But is it always the person with the best hand who wins a game of poker? Not at all! There are things that a player can observe about the other players—as well as things he or she can do to influence what the other players think and do—that affect the outcome of the game. Playing twice as many hands of poker doesn't double your odds of winning. In fact, if you are a novice player, it probably doubles your odds of going broke!

If we were to adhere solely to the numbers-game approach to selling, we would throw an equal amount of time and resources at every opportunity—conducting needs analyses, doing product demonstrations, and submitting proposals—with no regard to which ones were more likely to actually close. But doesn't your gut or your personal experience tell you that it's not just the *quantity* of the steps you take that determines your success?

All you have to do is observe top sales performers in most any sales situation. Generally, they are not the busiest, nor do they work the longest hours. They are the most effective and successful because of the *quality* of their work, not just the quantity. It's not the number of meetings they conduct but what they accomplish *at* those meetings that really matters.

As you set your sales goals—or as your goals are set for you—give some thought to what you might change about *how you sell* that would make you better equipped to attain them. Evolving as a sales professional requires more than just a firm resolve to "do more;" it requires us to learn to "do different" in order to produce different results.

Planning and Managing Your Sales Activity

Consistently reaching or exceeding your revenue goals requires thought, planning, and good old-fashioned hard work. It takes a lot of business development activity to find enough new opportunities to build an opportunity portfolio (pipeline) large enough to ensure that you reach your desired sales results. In the workshops that my company, Sales Excellence, Inc., conducts, we use a tool called a sales activity planning sheet (as shown in Figure 1.1 on page 9) to help participants develop a plan to ensure that they reach their sales goals.

Translating Your Results Goals into Portfolio Goals

To be successful, a certain level of sales activity is absolutely required. When you use a tool like the sales activity planning sheet, you can translate your results goals into portfolio goals, and from there into activity goals. The top section of the planning sheet simply defines how much additional sales revenue you will need to produce in order to reach your revenue goal by a certain date.

The middle section helps you determine how much potential revenue you need to be tracking in your opportunity portfolio in order to reach your revenue goal. You use the current average length of your sales cycles to figure out the date by which your portfolio needs to reach its target level. Then you use your current average deal size to determine how many new engagements you will need to identify each week to reach your portfolio goals. Once you have your portfolio goals laid out, then you can calculate the business development activity levels that will be required to achieve them.

Translating Your Portfolio Goals into Activity Goals

Using your best judgment and your historical performance, consider how many new prospective client meetings you typically have to conduct to find one new opportunity. If it typically takes you three face-to-face meetings with brand-new prospects to find one viable opportunity, for example, your conversion rate is 3:1. Also estimate how many new telephone connections it takes to book a meeting and how many new prospect approaches it takes to connect with a new prospect by phone. If you run the math, you can establish a good estimate of the sales activity required to reach your sales results goals.

Sometimes these numbers can be a little intimidating. If the number of calls you need to make or meetings you need to hold seems overwhelming or simply not possible, dial it back a bit. Don't scare yourself into inaction. I find that if you do this type of planning and then track your actual results, you are usually more successful at each step than you originally think. It's important to remember that your closure rate and conversion rates are not cast in stone. You can improve your conversion rates on telephone calls, new client meetings, and every other sales activity. The results-based selling method is dedicated to this objective.

In Chapter Three, we introduce a number of tools to help you track your success as well as many techniques that will make your business development efforts more effective. As you improve your conversion rates, you may choose to spend a little less time on business development,

Sales Activity Planning Sheet

Results Goals:

Revenue Goal: $ _2,000,000._ by (date) _Dec. 31_.

Revenue to Date: $ _800,000._. Additional Revenue Needed: $ _1,200,000._.

Portfolio Goals:

Target Opportunity Portfolio Value: $ _3,600,000._.

Total Number of Opportunities Needed : _12_.

Currently Have: _4_. New Opptys Needed: _8_.

All New Opptys Needed by (Date): _June 30_.

Weeks Left: _12_. New Opptys Needed per Week: _.75_.

Activity Goals:

New Prospective Client Meetings per Week: _3_.

New Telephone Conversations per Week: _12_.

New Prospect Approaches per Week: _36_.

Current Estimated Closure Rate

_3_ : 1

Current Avg. Deal Size

$ _300,000._

Current Avg. Sales Cycle

_178_ Days

Current Estimated Conversion Rates

_4_ : 1

_4_ : 1

_3_ : 1

Available at: **SalesExcellence.com**

Determine how much additonal sales revenue you will need by the end of your fiscal year.

Estimate your current closure rate to calculate how much potential revenue you will need in your portfolio.

Use your current average deal size to determine how many opportunities you need to be tracking.

Use the length of your average sales cycle to determine when you need to have these new opportunities identified and "in process."

Estimate your current conversion rates to calculate how many meetings, telephone conversations, and approaches it will take to reach your goals.

Figure 1.1 Sales Activity Planning Sheet

or you can maintain your aggressive activity levels and build your opportunity portfolio that much larger and that much faster.

Measuring and Managing Your Sales Results

Making more telephone calls and holding more meetings is certainly one way to increase your sales results. If the sales activity planning sheet reveals that you need to increase your business development activity in order to reach your goals, then you'll need to make the time to do the additional work. But also give some thought to how you could improve the results you get from your activity.

Let's take a closer look at the scenario in Figure 1.1. What if it were possible for you to increase your average deal size from $300,000 to $360,000? If everything else were unchanged, that alone would increase revenue by 20 percent! What if you could shorten that 178-day average sales cycle to 160 days? Yes, that would require shaving an average of 18 days off of every opportunity, but it would free up 10 percent of your time to invest in new opportunities and drive more revenue. What if you could improve your closure rate from 3:1 (33 percent) to 2.5:1 (40 percent)? That would be another 20 percent increase. All combined, these improvements could produce a whopping 50 percent boost in sales revenue without increasing your business development activity by even *one* phone call!

At the end of the day, increasing gross revenue is the result we all want to achieve. But if our only gauge for measuring our progress toward that objective is how much more revenue we need—and the only way we have to influence or impact that number is how many phone calls we make or meetings we conduct—we are completely missing the greatest opportunity to maximize our sales results. We need to look at the indicators that lead directly to increasing our revenue results using what I call a cause-and-effect model as shown in Figure 1.2.

There are actually only three ways to increase revenue. Fortunately, we can measure and proactively manage all three. They include:

1. Deal Size. The total dollar value of the customer transaction. This includes all the dollars your customer spends with you for a *discrete* (one-time) transaction or that they commit to spending by signing a contract to buy products or services over a specified period of time. In the food service industry, deal size is often called the *average ticket*. In retail it might be *sales per customer visit*. In any case, it's how much revenue a given transaction represents to your company.

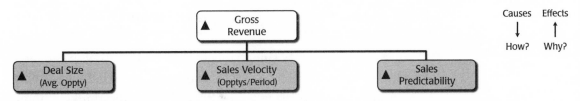

Figure 1.2 The Three Ways to Increase Revenue

2. Sales Velocity. How fast sales opportunities move through your sales pipeline or how many flow through in any given period of time. For big-ticket sales, this is usually measured by the number of days in a sales cycle, but velocity is also determined by the number of opportunities you can manage simultaneously at any given time. If you sell in a *flow* environment—where your customer commits to buying a predetermined quantity of products from you each month—it could be referred to as *sales volume.*

3. Sales Predictability. The number of opportunities that you expect to come to closure compared to the number that actually do close *when* you expected them to. This is often referred to as *closure rate* or *success rate.* Sales predictability is what determines the accuracy of sales forecasts.

* * *

These three variables can and should become the metrics we use as key performance indicators (KPIs) for measuring the results of our sales efforts because every increase in gross revenue is a direct result of an improvement in one of these three measures. If you want to increase revenue, begin to focus on growing the size of each opportunity, managing more opportunities at a time and closing them faster so you can prioritize your investment of time and energy on the opportunities that are most likely to close in a timely manner. That's what the results-based selling method is all about.

Why Measuring and Managing Results Work

There is a well-known business principle that states, "If you can measure it, you can manage it." When you begin measuring something you naturally start focusing your attention on it and thinking about how to improve it. The instant a salesperson or a sales team begins measuring and managing the metrics of deal size, velocity, and predictability, each person on the team starts to think about how to make each sales transaction a little bit bigger, how to make every transaction happen a little bit faster, and how to be a little more certain that opportunities will come to closure when we expect they will.

Managers who are so inclined can even attach rewards and incentives to these key measures to help reinforce the right behavior. But it's not always the cash bonuses, the trips, or the public recognition that drives sales behavior. Changes in behavior are driven by changes in thinking. The way salespeople think is shaped by the conversations they have with their sales managers, the questions their managers ask them, and the questions they ask themselves.

When I lead a results-based selling workshop, my objective is to teach the skills necessary for sales professionals to go out and effect major changes in their sales results. But in addition to transferring knowledge, I also have to cause a major shift in thinking. Of course, we all need to think about the consistency of our business development activity. But once we find an opportunity, we should begin to focus on the three objectives of deal size, velocity, and predictability by asking ourselves these three important questions:

1. How can I make this opportunity 10 or 20 percent bigger?
2. How can I close this opportunity one or two months sooner?
3. How can I be a little more certain that this opportunity will actually close when I think it will?

These three objectives can sometimes be at odds with one another. A bigger deal often moves through your pipeline slower, not faster. Managing more deals spreads your sales resources thinner and could have a negative impact on predictability. You will have to use your own best judgment to know when to try to make a deal bigger versus taking a smaller deal off the table sooner as well as how to invest your time to maximize your results.

Maximizing Deal Size, Velocity, and Predictability

Now that we have discussed the three ways to maximize your sales results—increasing deal size, maximizing sales velocity, and improving sales predictability—the next logical question is, "How do you do that?" There are numerous ways that each of these three measures can be influenced.

One way to increase deal size is to improve price integrity by minimizing discounts and other price concessions. One way to increase sales velocity is to focus on shortening sales cycles by accelerating both your business development process and your customer's buying process. An example of the major causes of deal size, velocity, and predictability are shown in Figure 1.3 on page 15.

Increasing Average Deal Size

What is the size of your average sales opportunity? The exact dollar figure is not what really matters. What matters is your ability to proactively maximize the size of each opportunity as you work it through your sales pipeline. But unless you know where you are now, it's fairly hard to gauge whether or not you are making any progress.

What if you could make every opportunity in your portfolio an average of 15 percent bigger? Wouldn't that be better than working 15 percent longer hours? If you're already working as long and as hard as you can, then increasing your average transaction size is one of the only ways you have to further grow your revenue. If it's been a while since you've thought about how to increase the average size of the opportunities in your pipeline—or if you've never thought about it before—let's take a look at some of the causes that influence deal size.

Increase Dollars at List Price. Look carefully at each opportunity you are currently working on. Determine the size of each one in terms of dollars at list price. Then, ask yourself, "What can I do today or over the course of this sales cycle to grow the size of this opportunity?" Don't try to sell your customer things they don't need, but always look for ways to increase the size of each deal.

Maybe you can expand the scope of your client's project to encompass multiple departments, cross-sell add-on products, or offer an extended service plan. Perhaps you could up-sell to the next larger size, the deluxe package, or the larger capacity. Of course, calling on larger companies and calling on people who are at higher levels within those companies are two effective ways to find larger sales opportunities.

Maintain Price Integrity. We have to make sure we don't allow too much of our revenue and profit to be eroded by discounts or other forms of price concessions. It seems almost too simple, but if we were to set a goal to reduce our average discount from 28 percent to 20 percent, we would automatically increase gross revenue by 8 percent!

Be very careful how you use buying incentives that don't directly reduce the purchase price of your product. Offering a "buy five at full price and get the sixth one free" promotion is the same as offering a 16 percent discount on all six. Discounts reduce your selling price, but they don't reduce your costs. They just erode your profit margin. Every dollar we *don't* give away in a discount or some other form of

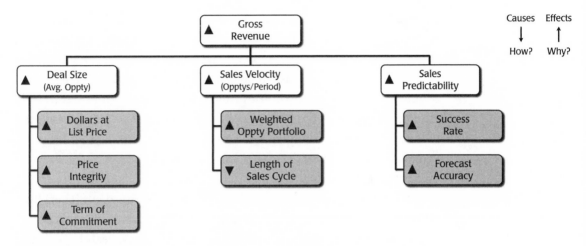

Figure 1.3 The Causes of Deal Size, Velocity, and Predictability

concession is a dollar of raw profit that we get to keep! In Chapter Nine, we talk more about maintaining price integrity through better negotiating skills.

Extend Your Customer's Term of Commitment. Another way of maximizing the total revenue of a potential sale is extending the duration of the customer's commitment. If you sell products in a flow environment, where your customer signs a contract to buy what you sell in certain quantities over a given period of time, then extending that contract from two years to three years would represent a 50 percent larger commitment. Also, look for opportunities to maximize the duration of service agreements or contracts.

Maximizing Sales Velocity

How many opportunities flow through your sales pipeline each quarter? The rate of opportunity flow is a function of *how many* deals you are currently working and *how fast* they move through the pipeline. I like to think of the sales opportunities in a pipeline as being similar to managing inventory. The quicker we can "turn" those opportunities, the sooner we can free up our time to invest in other opportunities.

If you track an average of 8 deals at a time and you could turn your portfolio of opportunities four times a year as opposed to only three, you could close 32 deals this year instead of 24. This would require reducing your average sales cycle from 120 days to 90 days, which is a very aggressive goal. But if you could accomplish that, you would increase gross revenue by 33 percent!

Of course, part of increasing the number of deals that flow through your sales pipeline each quarter is expanding your capacity to manage more deals at a time. The concepts, techniques, and tools in this book are specifically designed to help you maximize your sales capacity.

Grow Your Weighted Opportunity Portfolio. Your weighted opportunity portfolio (pipeline) is the dollar value of all the deals you are currently working on "weighted" by the probability that each one will come to closure. To grow your portfolio, you will need to either add more opportunities or improve the probability of the opportunities you already have. Chapter Three is dedicated to finding more sales opportunities, and Chapter Five is focused on measuring and improving the probability of each one.

Shorten Your Sales Cycle. The length of your sales cycle is determined by the length of your business development process *plus* the length of your customer's buying process. Anything we can do to compress either of these will help us shorten our overall sales cycle and thereby increase sales velocity. Chapter Three speaks to compressing your business development process, while Chapters Five and Six focus on accelerating your customer's buying process.

Improving Sales Predictability

Out of all the deals you tried to close last month, how many actually did close when you thought they would? Your overall success rate and the accuracy of your forecasts are vitally important metrics to track as you seek to improve the predictability of your sales results. There is some value in measuring how well we've done in the past, but what is more important is focusing on how to improve our success rate and forecast accuracy in the future. Then, we can use past and present performance as a benchmark to measure our improvement going forward.

Improve Your Success Rate. Our success rate is determined by the number of deals we *did* close, divided by the number of deals we *tried to* close. The key is not investing your time and sales resources trying to close every opportunity. We should determine which opportunities *can* close, which ones we have a good chance of winning, and which ones offer the greatest return on our investment.

Of all the opportunities in which you were up against a direct competitor, what portion of those did you end up winning? If you can determine who you lost to and why you lost, perhaps you can improve your odds in the future. Sometimes a customer decides *not* to buy because a project or initiative gets cancelled or is put on hold. As you learn to better qualify opportunities, you'll spend less time working on deals that never come to closure.

Improve Forecast Accuracy. What portion of the business that closed last month was accurately forecasted to close *last month?* That doesn't count what business closed that was originally forecasted to close the month before. This is what I refer to as "slippage." I realize that as long as you hit your numbers, nobody cares which month a particular deal was originally forecasted to close. But if we want to improve forecast accuracy, we have to begin by measuring what business did not close when it was originally forecasted to close. Then we can try to figure out why it didn't close, so we can learn to forecast more accurately in the future.

* * *

I realize that tracking numbers doesn't close deals. However, proactively influencing the size, velocity, and predictability of the deals you *do* close gives you tremendous leverage to improve your sales results. Focusing on these variables can help you make the most of every opportunity.

You won't be able to grow every deal. You won't be able to accelerate every buying process. But if you are aware of these things and at least try to maximize each opportunity, you will be shocked at what a difference you can make.

Tying Selling Skills to Sales Results

Focusing on deal size, velocity, and predictability can have a huge impact on how a salesperson—or an entire sales team—thinks and behaves. But once an individual or a team determines that they want to reduce their average discount rate, for example, they might need to further develop their negotiation skills to accomplish that goal. Figure 1.4 shows the cause-and-effect model extended downward one more level. It shows some of the factors that contribute to increasing dollars at list price, price integrity, term of commitment, etc.

This model also shows how the various skill sets of the sales profession correlate to maximizing your sales results. In this way, this model serves as a diagnostic tool that provides individuals and sales leaders with insight into what type of training or coaching might be required to help themselves or their team reach their revenue goals.

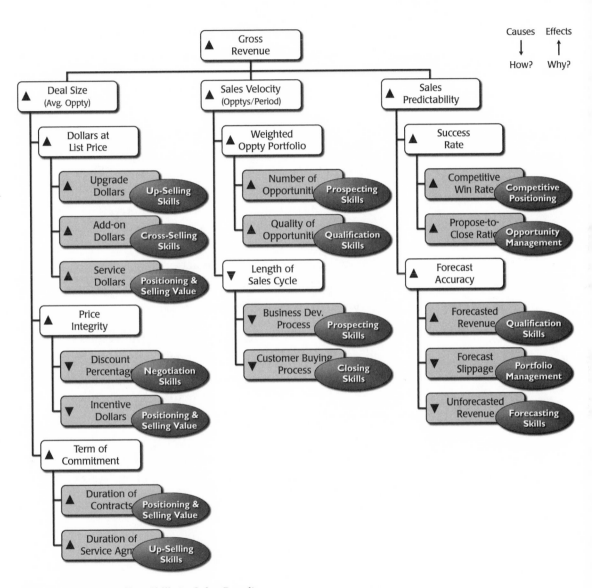

Figure 1.4 Tying Selling Skills to Sales Results

As you work your way through the rest of this book, you'll find chapters dedicated to each of these important skills as well as how to use them to get results.

* * *

In Chapter Ten, as we discuss how to implement the results-based selling method in your sales environment, I introduce a five-step process for setting and achieving your sales results goals. These five steps are:

> **Step one:** Determine where you are now.
> **Step two:** Decide where you want to be in the future.
> **Step three:** Develop your plan of action.
> **Step four:** Execute your plan.
> **Step five:** Measure your results.

This five-step process is the foundation of the results-based approach and will be a vital component in helping you reach the goals you set as you move forward. For now, just begin thinking about the kinds of sales results you would really like to achieve if anything were possible. Your plan of action will become clear as we talk about the various concepts and skills involved in the results-based selling method. Now let's move on to Chapter Two, where we talk about how to use the results-based approach to help your customers achieve their desired business results.

Helping Your Customers Achieve Their Desired Business Results

Working with customers can sometimes be frustrating or even downright exasperating. Just when you think you know what to expect, they move in an entirely different direction. At first glance, the decisions they make—or don't make—can seem almost nonsensical. The reason for the disconnect is that there is a big difference between how a salesperson sees the world and how a prospective customer sees the world.

If we take a step back and observe, we'll actually see that our customers are a lot like we are. Customers—and especially the executives and managers we deal with—are motivated and driven by their own desired outcomes and results. They don't buy our products for the reasons we think they should. If they decide to buy something, they buy for their reasons, not ours.

We have to accept that we can't control our customers. All we can do is seek to understand them and learn how to influence their thinking and behavior. Spending a little time to better understand how and why customers buy can pay huge dividends.

In this chapter, we concentrate on applying the results-based selling approach in order to help our customers achieve their desired business goals. This will involve digging deeply into how customers think, what drives their buying behavior, and the reasons *why* customers buy in the first place. We also investigate *how* customers buy so we can better understand their buying process and how they will use our products and services to achieve their business objectives. Last, we examine the context of a buying decision, how that influences our customer's thinking and behavior, and why understanding the context is so critically important to our success.

Becoming Customer Focused

I still vividly remember how excited I was when I took my first sales job. I knew that if success in the selling profession was based on hard work, I could make it happen. It didn't matter to me what I was selling. I believed that if I worked hard enough, surely I could find *somebody somewhere* who wanted to buy it.

My first year in sales was horrible. Actually, that might be too subtle a word for it. It was a disaster! I remember concluding about halfway through that first year that *nobody anywhere* wanted to buy what I was trying to sell. Have you ever felt that way? I didn't realize it at the time, but I was actually closer to the truth than I was when I started.

Looking back on things, I am grateful for the experience because at some point I realized what I consider to be the most important truth of selling: Nobody wants to buy your product or service. What they want are the *results* they can achieve by using what you sell to pursue their own goals and objectives. Once I learned that and began to look at the world from my customer's perspective, my sales results began to multiply exponentially.

I have come to firmly believe that there is no inherent value to our customers in our product and services solutions. The real value comes in how they use our solutions to achieve their desired business and personal results. In fact, our customers probably don't care about—or even want—the solution. What they want are the results. So I'd like to propose a somewhat radical idea. Why don't we quit trying to sell them solutions? Let's start *selling results!*

The Results-Based Approach to Selling

The results-based selling method is founded on the belief that to get the sales results *you* want, you have to help your customers get the business results *they* want. This means that you have to understand what your customer's desired business results are before you start selling your solution. This requires an approach that is quite different from the way many salespeople have been taught to sell.

If you've been trained to present to your prospective client before you have an interactive conversation, this approach will seem a little strange to you. If you've been told that knowing your product and transferring that product knowledge to your customer is the most important part of your job, then this method will require a substantial change in thinking. The results-based approach to selling is diagnostic in nature and stands in stark contrast to the ever-popular "broadcast" manner of selling that many customers have to endure far too often.

Getting out of Broadcast Mode

According to the broadcast approach to selling, our job is to do whatever is required to get an audience with our prospective customer, and once we get there, we present "who we are and what we do," as well as all the different solutions we bring to the table. The broadcast approach is like shooting up in the air and hoping that a duck will fly over. If you shoot enough times, you might eventually hit something, but you'll go through a ton of ammunition to do it.

If you are lucky, your prospective client might say, "Hold on there. Go back to slide 276 for a minute. I think I saw something there that might help us solve a problem we have." Sometimes you *will* hit a duck! However, if we just broadcast to our prospective clients and expect them to connect the dots between our capabilities and their business objectives, we are taking a huge risk. They usually don't know enough about all the different ways our products and services can be implemented or used to make the connection. That's our job to do!

Adopting the Results-Based Approach

The results-based approach takes a little more work and a little more time, but the payback is well worth the effort. You will need to invest some time reading about your prospect's company on their Web site. You might decide to type the name of one or two of their key executives into an online search engine to see what comes up. You could find a recent news article or press release that would give you some insight into what's going on in their business.

Once you get your customer on the phone or walk into a meeting, you'll start by asking a few important and relevant questions. You won't be worried about impressing them with all the facts and information about *you* and your company. Instead, you will impress them with what you've taken the time to learn about *them*. Your objective will be to learn about their business, their goals, and the challenges they currently face so you can position what you sell as a tool they can use to achieve their desired results.

Why This Approach Works

When we focus on helping our customers achieve their desired results, two very important things happen:

1. We Understand More. When we get a more accurate diagnosis of our customer's current situation and the goals and objectives they are trying to accomplish, we can ensure that whatever solution we might choose to propose is a perfect fit. We can better qualify opportunities and thus better manage our time by working on the best opportunities, which will significantly improve our success rate. We can also uncover many of the potential obstacles or potholes so that we can address them before they become objections.

2. Our Customers Feel More Understood. When our customers don't have to sit through the endless slide show of "who we are" or an exhaustive list of our product's features and functions, they have a chance to participate in the conversation. The discussion is about them, not us. When we use the results-based approach, we more effectively differentiate ourselves from our competition—not just by *what* we sell, but by *how* we sell. Our customers also feel more confident about what we propose. They have participated in the diagnosis; therefore, they have much more faith in the prescription.

* * *

Both of these benefits are significant, but more important than our need to understand is our customer's need to feel understood. If your customer doesn't feel that you are willing to slow down and listen to them, learn about their business, and come up with a joint plan of how to move forward, they'll probably keep looking for some other vendor who will take the time to make them feel understood.

Thinking Like a Customer

In my work as a keynote speaker and workshop leader, I have the opportunity to meet some of the most successful sales professionals from leading companies all over the world. There is one characteristic that I consistently find among top performers everywhere: They really understand their customers.

Some of the best salespeople I know are those who previously worked in the industry they now sell to before they entered the selling field. This makes sense, doesn't it? If you once held a similar role to the person you are selling to, you would have quite an advantage in comprehending all the expectations and constraints that they are faced with on a daily basis. Wouldn't you?

Most of us have never held the actual job that our prospective customers currently hold. Nevertheless, we should try to learn as much about their job as we can. We should try to learn who they report to, their primary and secondary responsibilities, how they are measured and compensated, as well as their current and future goals and objectives.

If we want to be highly effective at attracting, satisfying, and retaining customers, then we need to literally start to think like our customers. My first book, *Think Like Your Customer* (McGraw-Hill 2005), was written specifically for this purpose. If you've never been a CFO, it might be difficult to fully understand how to think *like* a CFO. But you can certainly learn to think *about* what CFOs think *about*. The better you understand how your customers think, the more you can influence their thinking and behavior.

What Customers Think About

As a sales professional, you probably spend most of your day thinking about your customers. But have you noticed that your customers don't spend their day thinking about you? They don't have time. They are too busy thinking about *their* customers. Depending on the job role they fill, they focus on their external customers, who buy the goods and services your customers bring to market; or their internal customers, who use or consume whatever it is they produce and deliver. If you sell through retail stores—or distributors who sell your products to other businesses or consumers—then helping them better serve *their* customers is an essential part of your job.

The executives we hope to sell to often spend a substantial percentage of their time thinking about their shareholders—yet a different category of customers—who "buy" a piece of the company (shares of stock) with plans to sell it at a profit some day. In this case, just as much as in the former, customer satisfaction and customer retention is vital.

In order to build the kind of strong partner-based relationships we all want to develop, we have to learn to look beyond what we do for *our* customers and begin to focus on how we help our customers help *their* customers. This is how we truly add value to our customer's business and help them achieve their desired business results.

Focusing on Customer Results

Using the results-based approach actually takes more work than just cold-calling, pitching your product, sending out a proposal, and asking for the order. It takes time and multiple conversations to really understand your customer and learn where they are now and where they would like to be in the future.

When we first encounter a prospective customer, we find them at a place I refer to as point A. This is their current state. If they are happy and content in the condition they are currently in and have no interest in exploring the possibilities of anything better, they probably won't buy a darn thing— and they shouldn't. But most of your prospective clients probably have all sorts of problems they want to solve, needs they'd like to fill, and goals and objectives they want to achieve.

The first step in engaging a customer is learning as much about their current state as possible. What we hope to find is some aspect of their current situation that they are not happy with or that they would like to change. It could be a need, pain, problem, challenge, initiative, goal, or objective. Whatever label they use, it represents a disparity between where they are now and where they would really like to be.

Hopefully, your prospective customer will be able to imagine (with your help) a different situation that they believe to be better than the situation they are in now. I refer to this desired future state as point C. This is the point at which your customer has solved their problem or achieved their desired results. Point C represents value to your customer. It could include almost anything. They might want to:

- Expand their market share to increase revenue.
- Cut costs to boost profitability.
- Improve worker productivity to increase throughput.
- Increase customer satisfaction to reduce client turnover.
- Improve quality to reduce product returns.

The list of desirable business results is virtually endless. Throw in the personal interests of your prospective customers, and the list is twice as long. These might include:

- A simpler way to place orders for the products you sell.
- Less hassle if they want to return something.
- Fresh ideas about how to use your solutions to improve their business.
- The comfort of dealing with a supplier who really knows their industry.

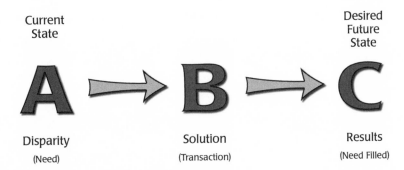

Current
State

Desired
Future
State

A ➡ B ➡ C

Disparity

(Need)

Solution

(Transaction)

Results

(Need Filled)

Figure 2.1 The Customer Results Model

In *Think Like Your Customer*, I introduced a model that has become the cornerstone of the results-based selling method. It's called the customer results model (shown in Figure 2.1).

What we need to do is determine if there is a gap between where our customer is now (A) and where they would really like to be (C) that we can fill with our solution, which I call B. We then position B as the vehicle or mechanism that helps them to get from A to C.

Sometimes it's not the actual product or service you sell that enables your customer to produce their desired business results. Often it's the way you deliver what you sell that makes all the difference and thus sets you apart from our competition. To win a competitive sale or unseat an incumbent vendor, you will have to help your customer identify or envision a C that you are uniquely qualified to help them achieve.

Understanding Why Customers Buy

Before your customer will take the steps to move from A to C, they will have to be driven to take action by some condition or circumstance. There are six different factors that influence why customers buy and that govern their desire to reach their imagined future state.

I call these action drivers. Understanding these six factors—as well as their importance to any particular person involved in a buying decision—is absolutely crucial for understanding why that customer would buy.

The action drivers include:

1. Motive
2. Urgency
3. Payback/Return
4. Means/Resources
5. Consequence(s)
6. Risk(s)

Motive

The first and most important action driver is motive: *Why* would your customer decide to buy? Without a good reason why, your customer will never seriously consider buying anything. It's not the motive to own your product (B) that drives your customer to take action. It's the motive to complete a project, execute a plan, or reach the higher-level goal that drives the buying decision. They are driven by the value of getting to point C.

Urgency

Individuals sometimes buy when they want to, but companies normally buy things only when they have to. The operative word in this sentence is *when*. If your customer can put off buying, switching vendors, or altering their scheduled order commitments, they probably will. Sometimes the delay is procrastination on the part of someone involved in the buying process. But often it's just good cash management. Why should they lay out money until they absolutely have to?

Your customer seldom has an urgency to buy—except in the rare case in which they have some money in their budget that will go away if it's not spent by the end of their fiscal year. The urgency that drives a purchase is the urgency to complete a project, achieve a goal, or arrive at point C at a certain time.

Payback/Return

From a business point of view, any purchase or investment is only as good as the return that comes from that investment. Before your customer will buy anything, they will have to believe that there is some payback that is worth more than the investment and the inherent risk of investing. Exploring payback or return helps your customer to *quantify* the value of reaching point C.

Means/Resources

Even if point C seems like nirvana to your customer, they can't use your B to get there without the means or the resources to pay for it and put it to use. This includes more than just having money in their budget. Think about all the resources your customer would need to make available in order to get to C, such as the staff to implement and use whatever product or service you sell them. Without sufficient resources, your customer can't take action and buy.

Consequence(s)

The most reliable action driver of all is the *consequence* to your customer if they don't get to point C when they need to get there. Consequences drive action. The lack of consequences promotes the status quo. If there is no consequence that motivates your customer to make a buying decision, don't be too surprised when they decide to do nothing.

Risk(s)

The first five action drivers move your customer to take action to get from A to C. Risk, however, is what makes your customer want to avoid taking any action at all. The funny thing about the way risk works in your customer's mind is that there doesn't have to be an actual risk to deter them from taking action. An imaginary risk will do just fine. We need to understand our customer's perception of the risks involved in moving forward if we want to understand why they would or wouldn't buy.

* * *

These six elements play a pivotal role in the results-based selling method. We refer to these action drivers many times throughout this book. They are vital for understanding why your customer would buy and for properly qualifying any sales opportunity. They are essential for effectively positioning your solution. I have also found that the overwhelming majority of objections you will ever hear from a prospective customer relate to a lack of motive, urgency, payback, resources, consequences, or too much perceived risk.

Positioning Your Solution

The technique of understanding our customer's point C *before* we position our B is what I call intelligent positioning, as shown in

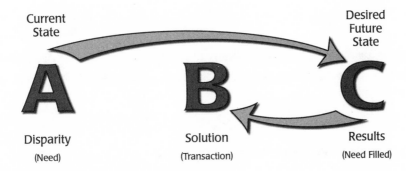

Figure 2.2 Intelligent Positioning

Figure 2.2. We use our knowledge of our customer's business and the goals they are trying to accomplish to establish exactly how to position our solution. This way we emphasize the capabilities of our solutions that lead directly to the results our clients want to accomplish without explaining all those features and benefits that may very well be irrelevant.

In the alphabet these three letters appear as A, B, C. But in the results-based approach to selling, we need to think about them starting with A, and then C, before we get to B.

This approach is quite a departure from positioning our solution based only on why it is better than our competitor's offering. The more time we spend talking about the capabilities of our solutions that don't really matter to our customer, the less they feel that we truly understand them or what they are trying to accomplish.

Your customers don't buy your product or service for all the things that it can do. They buy it for a few things that it can do to help them achieve one or more specific outcomes or results. A "data dump" of all your product's features and functions is not only time consuming and monotonous, but it can actually intimidate your customer and make them feel that your solution is too big and too complex. The next thing they'll tell you is, "We don't need it to do all that. We only need about 30 percent of it. Can we get a 70 percent discount?"

We should always remember that our B has relevance only as it relates to helping our customer arrive at point C. Without a desirable C that our B can help them get to, our B is not a solution at all. It's just another product or service that nobody wants to buy.

Fitting Your Solution to Your Customer's C

At some point, it becomes appropriate to position your solution (B) as the means to help your customer get from A to C, but you should resist the temptation to start positioning too early. The longer you wait to propose your B, the more opportunity you have to gather information that will help you differentiate yourself from your competitors. If you begin positioning too early, it can be very difficult to change your customer's perception later on.

Figure 2.3 shows three different strategies for fitting your solution to your customer's C and differentiating yourself from your competition.

One way to position your solution is by how much bigger and better it is than what your competitor offers. While this seems like a sound approach, it can be risky, because if either solution will work, why should your client care how much bigger and better yours is?

Another way to position your solution is to take the opposite of the bigger and better approach. This is where you position your solution as a tighter fit for your customer's needs. This can sometimes be an effective approach, but be careful. Your customer might expect yours to be less expensive.

The third approach is to try to reshape your customer's point C so that your offering does everything they need it to do, but your competitor's offering won't. Always remember that while you sell a B, what your customer buys is a C. What makes your solution superior is how well it

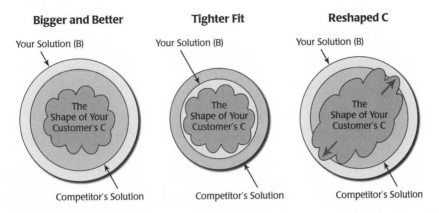

Figure 2.3 Fitting Your Solution to Your Customer's C

fits your customer's desired point C. If you go into a sales opportunity focused only on beating the competition, you've already lost.

Repositioning Your Solution

Over time, point A and point C will frequently change. Your customer's current state will be different tomorrow than it is today, and their perception of the ideal future state can change even more rapidly than that. Point C can shift as your customer explores all the possibilities that might be available to them. Also keep in mind, as you meet more of the people who are involved in the buying process, that each person can have a very different opinion of the ideal point C.

If we understand this new definition of C, and stay grounded in the results-based approach, we can reposition our B any way we need to. Once we locate the new desired future state and the different results our customers want to achieve, the ideal position for B becomes rather obvious, as shown in Figure 2.4.

No product or service can help your customer achieve *every* outcome or result they might desire, but you can certainly emphasize

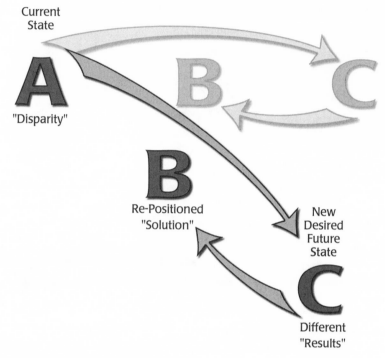

Figure 2.4 Repositioning Your Solution

different aspects of what it *will* do, as needed. If you practice intelligent positioning as you work with more of the people within your customer's organization, you can reposition your solution for each new person you meet. It's the same product or service, but how you position it—based on the business or personal results each person wants to achieve—can vary substantially.

Positioning to Maximize Customer Results

Each person who plays a role in your customer's buying process can have a unique perception of point A and the ideal point C. It is often

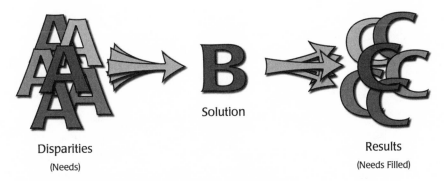

Solution

Disparities
(Needs)

Results
(Needs Filled)

Figure 2.5 Positioning to Maximize Customer Results

surprising how differently two people working within the same company can think. The way we tie it all together and propose a great solution that maximizes our customer's results is to:

1. Understand point A for as many of the people involved as we are able to meet.
2. Identify as many individual C's as we think we can honestly and reliably deliver.
3. Position our B to turn as many A's into as many C's as possible, as shown in Figure 2.5.

Rethinking Your Sales Process

Making the transition from selling products and services to selling business results requires a number of fundamental changes in how we think about our role as salespeople. If our job is to help our customer get from point A to point C, we have to understand more than just *why* our prospective customer would buy our solutions. We also have to figure out *how* they could buy our solution and use it to achieve their desired results.

Those who have read *Think Like Your Customer* may remember the chapter called "The Sales Process—Redefined." For those who haven't read it, let's do a quick review. Please take a look at the sample sales process depicted in Figure 2.6, making note of the words "things we do" and "things they do" on the far left. This is not *your* sales process. Nor am I suggesting it should be. I use this model simply to illustrate a point and to ask a few very important questions.

Is it possible that we could work through every single step shown in every stage of this sample sales process (in the upper boxes) and still not close a sale? Absolutely! That happens all too frequently. Doesn't it? Now, let's ask a different question. If your customer took all the steps they needed to take in their buying process (such as those in the lower boxes) but we forgot to take a couple of the steps in our sales process, could we still accept the order? Of course!

This is one of the most sobering truths of selling. We can't make our customers buy no matter how hard we sell. All we can do is try to understand why they would buy—and how they could buy if they wanted to—and use that knowledge as we lead them through their own buying process.

The major takeaway from this discussion is that once we engage with our customer, everything we do in *our* sales process should be done with the intention of helping our customer take a step they need to take in *their* buying process. I call this selling with specific intent. Anything we do that doesn't lead to our customer taking the next step in their process could be a complete waste of time and energy. Now let's take this discussion to the next level.

The Two Major Phases of Your Sales Process

Our overall sales process actually consists of two phases. The first phase includes all the things that we do to discover, research,

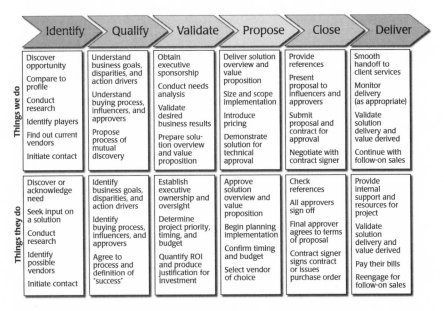

	Identify	Qualify	Validate	Propose	Close	Deliver
Things we do	Discover opportunity Compare to profile Conduct research Identify players Find out current vendors Initiate contact	Understand business goals, disparities, and action drivers Understand buying process, influencers, and approvers Propose process of mutual discovery	Obtain executive sponsorship Conduct needs analysis Validate desired business results Prepare solution overview and value proposition	Deliver solution overview and value proposition Size and scope implementation Introduce pricing Demonstrate solution for technical approval	Provide references Present proposal to influencers and approvers Submit proposal and contract for approval Negotiate with contract signer	Smooth handoff to client services Monitor delivery (as appropriate) Validate solution delivery and value derived Continue with follow-on sales
Things they do	Discover or acknowledge need Seek input on a solution Conduct research Identify possible vendors Initiate contact	Identify business goals, disparities, and action drivers Identify buying process, influencers, and approvers Agree to process and definition of "success"	Establish executive ownership and oversight Determine project priority, timing, and budget Quantify ROI and produce justification for investment	Approve solution overview and value proposition Begin planning implementation Confirm timing and budget Select vendor of choice	Check references All approvers sign off Final approver agrees to terms of proposal Contract signer signs contract or issues purchase order	Provide internal support and resources for project Validate solution delivery and value derived Pay their bills Reengage for follow-on sales

Figure 2.6 The Sales Process—Redefined

approach, connect with, and engage new sales opportunities. This is what I refer to as our business development process, which we cover in depth in Chapter Three.

After we meet with, qualify, and engage a new client, the second phase of our process begins. From that point on, *our* sales process should be totally centered on helping our customer to define and work through *their* buying process. In some instances, our approach is what initiates their buying process. But in other cases, they could have started considering and evaluating solutions well before we came along, as illustrated in Figure 2.7.

The steps we take in our business development process are mostly within our own control. If one prospect won't take our phone call or doesn't want to meet with us, we simply move on to the next. However, once we find a new sales opportunity and choose to engage, progress happens only when our customer takes a step in their buying process.

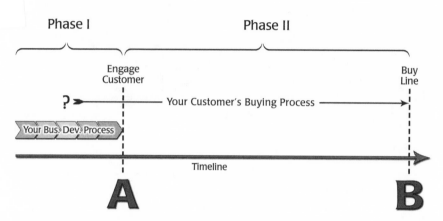

Figure 2.7 The Two Major Phases of a Sales Process

Understanding Your Customer's Buying Process

When we think about the sales opportunities we are currently engaged in—or when we sit down to strategize with our manager—we tend to ask ourselves the *wrong* question. We look at an opportunity and ask, "What do *we* need to do to close this deal?" Unfortunately, we could do 47 things and still not close a sale because it's not the actions we take to sell something but the actions our customer takes to buy something that ultimately bring an opportunity to closure.

To make the transition to the results-based selling approach, take a step back and instead of focusing on what you are going to do next in your sales process, ask yourself these four important questions:

1. What Will Be Involved in This Particular Buying Process? Every buying process is a little different. Each company has their own set of policies and procedures they use when buying something. You need to understand all the steps and the people involved in the buying process for each significant opportunity. To help bring more clarity to your endeavor, ask yourself the question, "What are all the things that would have to happen before this customer could buy?"

2. Where Is the Customer within Their Buying Process? When you engage your customer at point A, they may already have taken some steps to evaluate solutions, obtain funding, or get approval for the project that your solution would be a part of. Figure out exactly where they are in their process by learning the answers to these two questions: "What has already happened in their buying process?" and "What still needs to happen?"

3. What Is the Next Reasonable Step the Customer Needs to Take? It is probably not reasonable for a new prospect to sign a $200,000 contract at the end of your first meeting—or even your second or third. You will need to determine what would be the next *reasonable* step in your prospect's buying process. Always think, "What should I ask my customer to do next?" Then think, "What would be the logical next step after that?" The better you understand what must take place going forward, the more effective you will be at leading your customer through their buying process.

4. What Can We Do to Help the Customer Take That Step? Once you have an understanding of your customer's buying process, where they are within their process, and what the next reasonable step should be, then you are ready to ask yourself, "What am I going to say or do on this next phone call or at this next meeting to help them take that step?" By going into each meeting or phone call with a clear plan of what you hope to accomplish based on your customer's buying process, you will increase your effectiveness exponentially.

Always keep your eyes and ears open for what may have changed since you last spoke or met with your client. Sometimes your plan might need to change right in the middle of the meeting. If that happens, revisiting these four questions will get you right back on track.

The Context of a Buying Decision

When a new prospective client approaches us—or when you find a client who is involved in some form of evaluation and buying process—it's only natural for you and your prospect to focus on what they want to buy. The tendency to broadcast is strong. Prospects, especially those who are individual contributors (such as lab technicians, design engineers, database administrators, etc.) are often very product-focused and have lots of questions about the solutions that you sell. In these situations, the conversation tends to revolve around the features and functions of your solutions.

Whether your prospect (we'll call him Clem) is doing his own fact-finding or his boss has asked him to determine the need for some new piece of equipment, he is focused on answering the question, "Do we need to buy something?" His attention is all wrapped up in the *purchase* aspect of the overall buying decision. But this is only one of several decisions that must be made before Clem's company will actually buy something.

If Clem, or the committee on which he sits, finds that there is a need to buy something, then his focus turns to selecting the best solution to fill that need. Once the committee determines the ideal solution, they will likely look at a number of different sources to select the vendor who can best deliver it. Figure 2.8 shows how these decisions link together as your customer works through the purchase, solution, and source aspects of their buying decision.

The assumption that we make too often is that someone (whom we have not met) has already decided that if Clem determines a need

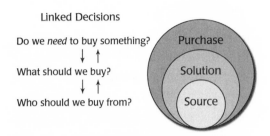

Figure 2.8 The Ingredients of a Buying Decision

for new equipment—and he finds the ideal solution and the ideal vendor—they will automatically be ready and able to buy. If you have any doubts, just ask Clem. He'll tell you emphatically, "Once I make my recommendation, my boss will place the order."

Sometimes Clem just tells us that they're going to buy so we'll start jumping through all his hoops, providing product literature and demonstrations, and showering him with mouse pads, coffee mugs, and T-shirts. Other times Clem really believes it! He may not realize that his boss—or his boss's boss—is considering dozens of projects and purchases. It's fine for Clem to assume that once he makes his recommendation his boss will automatically take action to buy, but we can't afford to assume that.

What we have to remember is that the purchase decision is actually just a small part of several larger decisions that have to be made—in many cases, without consulting or even notifying Clem or the committee. We have to understand the context that surrounds the buying decision if we want to really understand how and why our customer would buy.

How the Context Affects the Buying Decision

Most purchases a company makes are tied to a project or an initiative that supports a plan to achieve a business goal or objective. A purchase decision is seldom made in a vacuum. Rather, a decision is made to move forward with a certain project, and thus the decision to buy certain products or services associated with the project is also made. Other times, management revamps their strategic plan, which eliminates a given project altogether, and the decision *not* to purchase the products or services tied to that project simply follows. Figure 2.9 shows how the purchase decision fits into the larger scheme of things.

When we think about why our customer would buy, we have to take into consideration why they would pursue a certain business goal or objective or why they would undertake a given project at this time. The context of the buying decision and the other higher-level decisions play a bigger role in whether your customer will purchase something than does finding the ideal solution or the ideal source to buy it from.

It is not uncommon for a member of a selection committee, or even the leader of a committee, to have no idea why their company would ultimately buy. They're often not privy to all the larger decisions at hand. Their job is to figure out *what* to buy and *who* to buy it from.

When we encounter a new sales opportunity, we should try to quickly determine whether it is a bottom-up sales opportunity—a potential purchase in search of a project that can hopefully be linked to a corporate goal. Or if it's a top-down sales opportunity—where goals, strategies, and plans are already established and the potential purchase is part of a project that is already approved, staffed, and funded.

To help your customer achieve their desired business results, you have to understand the context of the buying decision and the ultimate business-level goals and objectives they are trying to achieve. This will entail meeting more of the people who will be involved in the overall buying process and who will be responsible for making the larger decisions. As Figure 2.9 illustrates, these decisions are typically made at the senior management or executive level. Take a good

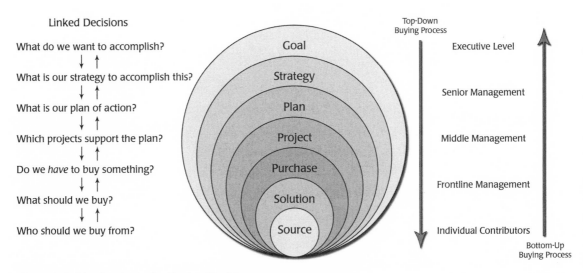

Figure 2.9 The Context of a Buying Decision

long look at this figure. We revisit this concept many times throughout this book.

* * *

In the coming chapters, we dig deeper into understanding and influencing how and why your customers buy. We discuss how to navigate your way through your customer's organization and meet more of the people—especially the executives—who will play key roles in any buying decision. We cover how to qualify sales opportunities and evaluate the likelihood that each of your opportunities will ultimately close.

Later on, we focus on how to help your customer define and work through their buying process. We also explore how to be more effective at selling to the senior-level executives. But next, let's talk about using the results-based selling method to fill our sales pipelines and improve both the quantity *and* the quality of new sales opportunities.

CHAPTER THREE

Mastering Your Business Development Process

Your sales results will ultimately be determined by a host of different factors. These include your effectiveness in qualifying opportunities, positioning and proposing your solution, and bringing business to closure. However, success in each of these areas is predicated on the assumption that you are able to find or identify enough viable sales opportunities to qualify, position, propose, and close to begin with.

Sales prospecting, which is often referred to as business development, is probably the most foundational of all professional selling skills. The number and the quality of the opportunities in your sales pipeline, your revenue results, and ultimately your income are largely determined by your success in business development. Fortunately, this is one area that most of the salespeople who attend my workshops are eager to improve in.

In this chapter, we begin by looking at the difference between marketing and prospecting and why your commitment to prospecting is so essential to producing consistent sales results. We explore the issue of time management and how to maximize the return on your investment of business development activity.

Later on in this chapter, we discuss how to create and use your own business development process, which will enable you to improve your results and accomplish more in less time. We also look at several different tools that you can use to plan and track your business development efforts as you work to build up your inventory of opportunities and improve the quality of your sales pipeline. This will lead directly to increased sales velocity and better predictability of sales results.

Inbound vs. Outbound Business Development

There are two different approaches that companies use to attract and find new sales opportunities: inbound business development (marketing) and outbound business development (prospecting). Marketing includes everything that your company does to cause an interested buyer to find you, such as print advertising, direct mail, seminars, trade shows, or driving traffic to your company's Web site. Marketing can be highly targeted to carry a specific message to a certain type of buyer. But for the most part, it involves casting a wide net in search of potential customers. When a prospective client responds, they become an inbound lead for a salesperson to follow up with.

Prospecting, on the other hand, is more about us finding them. It is outbound in nature, and it usually involves a fair amount of work for the sales professional. For some of us, it requires venturing outside our comfort zone and running the risk of being rejected at some point along the way. Therefore, it is very tempting to just wait for somebody in the marketing department to provide us with leads. This can be a problem.

Inbound Business Development

In my workshops, I meet thousands of sales professionals every year. Unfortunately, I almost never meet anyone who is happy with the quality or quantity of the leads they receive from their marketing department. Many salespeople feel that they either aren't given enough leads, or the leads they do get aren't highly qualified. Ironically, the marketing people who attend my workshops are equally frustrated because their salespeople won't even follow up on the leads they *do* provide. There is a reason for this.

Some inbound leads can become great opportunities. But by their very nature, there are several characteristics of these prospects that make them—shall we say—less than ideal:

1. We Almost Always Have to Start at the Bottom. When you receive an inbound lead, who is it that usually contacts you? Is it the chairman of the board? How about the vice president of finance? No, it's usually someone at the individual contributor level or occasionally a frontline manager. It's Clem, who we met in Chapter Two.

Clem is our friend! He can usually help us learn more about his company than we can learn by reading their Web site. He might even be able to open some doors for us. But in most cases, he can't make a buying decision. More often, he is a recommender or a professional gatherer of information. By starting with Clem, we have to sell our way up from the bottom.

2. It Is Often Very Late in the Game. When Clem contacts us, we frequently find that our customer is already in the late stages of a selection process. Clem's company sends him out to find three or four vendors to offer competitive bids that they can compare to the proposal they've received from the vendor they already want to buy from. Engaging late in the process is always challenging because the customer already has a mature vision of point C and of the ideal B. It is usually very difficult to influence their evaluation criteria or to differentiate ourselves from our competition on anything other than price.

3. Sometimes There Isn't a Game. Clem is an expert tire kicker. He often feels it's his job to scour the market for products or services that might be useful to his company even if there are no related projects or initiatives being considered. Engaging a client early can be great! It's often easier to get access to the people who may become influencers and approvers in some future buying decision. But all too often Clem contacts us and expects us to take the time to educate him on everything we do just in case his company has a need one day.

4. We Frequently Get Stuck Selling to One Person. When Clem calls us, he typically believes it's his job to be the gatekeeper and not allow us to talk to anybody but him. He thinks he gets to tell us who we can or can't meet with. This is a very troublesome dynamic which can be extremely difficult to overcome. If we can't understand the context of the buying decision—or what point C represents to the other people involved—it is almost impossible to properly position our solution and build the relationships needed to win the business.

5. If They Are Looking at Us, They Are Probably Looking at Others Too. By nature, inbound opportunities are highly competitive. If Clem contacts us, he'll probably be contacting other vendors too. We sometimes find ourselves trying to sell by submitting a request for proposal (RFP) and hoping they like what they read. Clem often feels that in order to be fair to all vendors, he can't be forthcoming or helpful to any of them.

* * *

As sales professionals, we want all the leads we can get. But as you can see, many leads turn into Clem-level interactions that can be both challenging and time consuming. In many cases, once an opportunity finds you, the deck is already stacked against you. My advice is, don't wait around for your marketing department to hand you your fate. Get out and create some additional opportunities on your own. Ensure your own success by mastering the process of outbound business development.

Outbound Business Development

Outbound business development takes work. It requires a certain level of ambition or motivation and a willingness to fail more times than you succeed. But certain characteristics of the opportunities you find by prospecting make them well worth the effort:

1. We Can Start at Any Level We Want. When we reach out to our prospect before they contact us, we don't have to start with Clem. That doesn't mean that we will always begin by calling the CEO (chief executive officer). We may want to talk to several other managers or executives to get a better understanding of their business before we approach the big boss. But we can begin our approach at whatever level we feel is appropriate. That way, when you branch out to meet more people within the organization, you can sell downward from the top.

2. We Can Often Engage Earlier in the Game. If we approach them, we can sometimes discover a sales opportunity early in the customer's overall buying process. Our approach may even be the trigger that initiates a selection and buying process. This gives us greater opportunity to influence and shape their vision of point C and their perception of the ideal B. Of course, some of the companies we approach will be content to stay at A. In other cases, our B may not be a good fit. But if we find an opportunity early on, we may be able to influence the scope of the project or even help define the selection criteria and the buying process.

3. We Can Approach Several People at Once. To avoid getting stuck selling to only one person, we can approach several different people who fill different roles all at the same time. If you sell application software, for example, you can approach the head of whichever department would ultimately use your software, the head of IT, and the head of finance simultaneously. This accelerates your business development process, which leads to shorter sales cycles, and enables you to more quickly broaden your relationship footprint.

4. We Tend to Get Far Less Interference from Gatekeepers. When we initiate contact and we call higher in our client's organization, we get far less push-back from Clem. If he hasn't yet been assigned the specific objective of evaluating potential vendors, Clem is far less threatened by our desire to meet the other people in his company. If we are successful at directly approaching and connecting with people higher in the company, we can sometimes eliminate the gatekeeper issue altogether.

5. We Can Become the Benchmark. When we uncover a potential opportunity before our competitors do, we have the opportunity to set the standard. If we meet and build relationships with enough of the influencers and approvers, every other vendor will be compared to us, and our solution will be the one that all the others are evaluated against.

* * *

It's true that you will invest some of your time researching and reaching out to companies who will not become qualified prospects, let alone new clients. But for all the reasons listed above—and because waiting around for good leads is just plain frustrating—outbound prospecting is a crucial part of maximizing your sales results. The question is, "How do you find or make the time for prospecting and how can you make sure the time you do spend produces the results you want?" Read on!

Managing Your
Business Development Activity

While most salespeople appreciate the importance of business development, there are two major challenges that we all seem to face: Either we don't do enough prospecting, or our prospecting efforts are inconsistent. Although we try to find the time to do the research, write the letters, and make the phone calls, something else always seems to come up.

If we allow this situation to linger, we can end up with an anemic sales pipeline half-filled with low-quality opportunities, some of which we'd be better off walking away from. The problem is that a salesperson won't walk away from an opportunity—even if they know it's a bad investment of their time and effort—unless they have another opportunity to walk toward. You can't make smart choices if you don't have any options.

Many of us want to do more prospecting, but it becomes a time management issue as we juggle all our other responsibilities. Some salespeople tell me that they spend as much as 90 percent of their time taking care of existing customers and other responsibilities, leaving very little time for prospecting. One thing is certain: There is no limit to what your existing clients will ask you to do if you make yourself available. But if we don't spend enough time at it or if we prospect in spurts, we never get comfortable enough to be really good at it.

Is it possible for you to be a little more efficient? Could you figure out how to do everything you need to do for your existing clients in only 80 percent of your time? If you could, that would leave you with 20 percent of your time for finding new opportunities instead of only 10 percent. By being just a little more efficient taking care of existing clients, you could *double* the amount of time you can invest in business development.

The Business Development Roller Coaster

Even more challenging than finding the time for business development is staying consistent with our prospecting activity. Every so often, perhaps following an annual sales kickoff, we get excited and decide to get busy prospecting for new opportunities. But once we identify a few new deals to work on and we start booking meetings, it's easy to take our eye off of prospecting and focus entirely on closing the business at hand. This is especially true during the last few weeks of each fiscal quarter.

As we give more attention to closing deals, our prospecting activity slows down or even drops off to nothing. Meanwhile, our revenue actually starts to increase as we close the deals we are working on.

As the next quarter begins, revenue starts to decline or dries up altogether, and we find ourselves with no new opportunities to work on. So, we get busy prospecting again. But because of the length of our sales cycle, it takes us 60, 90, or 120 days to start putting up numbers again.

Your revenue results follow your prospecting activity almost exactly, but they follow on a lag. That lag is determined by the length of your sales cycle. The peaks and valleys in your prospecting activity create peaks and valleys in your revenue results. Due partly to inconsistent prospecting efforts, we have good months and bad months, good quarters and bad quarters, and even good years and bad years. I call this the business development roller coaster, as shown in Figure 3.1.

Normalizing Your Business Development Results

One of the primary objectives of the results-based selling method is to normalize (smooth out) your revenue results by being more consistent

Figure 3.1 The Business Development Roller Coaster

with your prospecting activity. Here are four important things you can do to reduce the effects of the business development roller coaster.

1. Plan Your Time and Prioritize Your Prospecting Activities. Set aside time for prospecting, and don't let your time be robbed from you. Schedule it on your calendar, shut off your e-mail and your cell phone, and get to work. This may mean that you have to stay at the office a little later the day before or plan to get into the office earlier the day after, but guard your prospecting time ferociously. No one else is going to guard it for you.

2. Develop a Reliable and Repeatable Process for Prospecting. If you have to reinvent the wheel every time you have a few minutes for prospecting, you'll never get anything done. Here is the all too common scenario.

It's late in the afternoon, and you've put out most of the fires of the day. Then, you think, "I should make a few prospecting calls." You look at your list and say, "Let's see, which company should I approach?" You pick one and think, "Who *within* the company should I try to reach?"

If you do have a name, then the question becomes, "Should I just pick up the phone and call? Or should I take a look at their Web site first? Maybe I should start by sending a letter. But that means I can send the letter today, but I can't call them until I allow a few days for the letter to get there." By the time you get it all figured out you're out of time. If this sounds familiar, you need a process for prospecting, which you will have before you finish this chapter.

3. Focus on Shortening Sales Cycles. Reducing the length of your average sales cycle may seem like a separate issue, but it actually has a huge effect on reducing the roller coaster effect and the lag between activity and results. Every day that you can shave off of any sales opportunity is one more day you can spend finding or closing the next opportunity. There are ideas for shortening sales cycles throughout this book.

4. Never Let Your Prospecting Activity Go Back to Zero. Make sure you do a little prospecting every week if not every day. Some salespeople prefer to set aside an entire morning. Others are more comfortable fitting calls in between the scheduled events in their day. Experiment with both and do what works best for you.

If your prospecting activity drops back to zero, then it is inevitable that your revenue will also drop back at some point in the future. You may be familiar with the acronym ABC which stands for "always be closing." Let me be the one to implore you to ABP—"always be prospecting." If you think about it, it is *impossible* to ABC if you don't ABP.

Your Business Development Process

One of the best things you can do to maximize your sales results is to design your own business development process. This is simply a series of steps and stages you work through to discover, research, approach, connect with, and engage new prospective clients.

As we discuss in Chapter Two, your business development process is the first phase of your sales cycle and is mostly within your control. I recommend creating and mastering a repeatable process that you can execute over and over again. As you get better at each step—and at working through the entire process—you can learn to move through your process faster, which creates momentum and shortens your overall sales cycles. Most of all, it gives you tremendous confidence as you prove to yourself that the next qualified sales opportunity is only a few action steps away.

Depending on your sales environment, your process should be designed to reflect how you find, identify, and engage new opportunities. If you work in what is often referred to as an inside sales environment and your sales leads are mostly inbound, the steps and stages of your process will be a little different from those for an outside salesperson. Figure 3.2 on page 59 shows an outbound business development process that we teach in our prospecting workshops.

These steps and stages might not be exactly what you do to find and engage new sales opportunities in your selling environment. You might need to make a few changes to this model before you can use it. Regardless of whether you decide to design your own or use this one as is, put your business development process to use starting today! Now let's walk through the five stages of this sample process and talk about the steps involved in each.

The Discover Stage

The first stage of an outbound business development (BD) process involves discovering new potential accounts and the individuals within those accounts who might play a role in a buying process. It can be very helpful to develop what I call a profile of an ideal client to use as a yardstick to evaluate prospects. Write down the characteristics and qualities of a great customer. That way you'll know exactly what you are looking for so you'll easily recognize it when you find it.

I encourage you to build an opportunity network made up of complementary vendors (salespeople who sell products different from yours to the same buyers you want to sell to) and industry contacts with whom you can swap names and maybe even collaborate on opportunities. A strong network can provide you with a regular supply of new prospective accounts as well as contacts within those accounts. Give some thought to who else is already selling to the specific people you need to be selling to. Reach out to them and see if they would like to work together for your mutual benefit.

From your database, create a living list of 10 or 12 target accounts to work on. When one falls off because you disqualified it for some reason, replace it with a new one. Once you have your list of target accounts, you'll need the names of the people who currently fill the roles you need to be selling to.

Use your networking contacts, your coworkers, Web research, newspapers, trade journals, and other news sources to build your list of names within each account. Be sure to check your own company data, such as sales records, service records, old contracts, mailing lists, and so forth. Also check with other people who work at your company who might know someone who works at one of your target accounts.

As you build up your list of contacts within each account, select five or six key executives who you will research and approach first. These should be the people who will likely play a key role in any future decision to buy the kinds of products or services you sell. Begin by focusing your efforts on these target contacts. Once you've reached out to contact them, you can move on to some of the other names you may have discovered along the way.

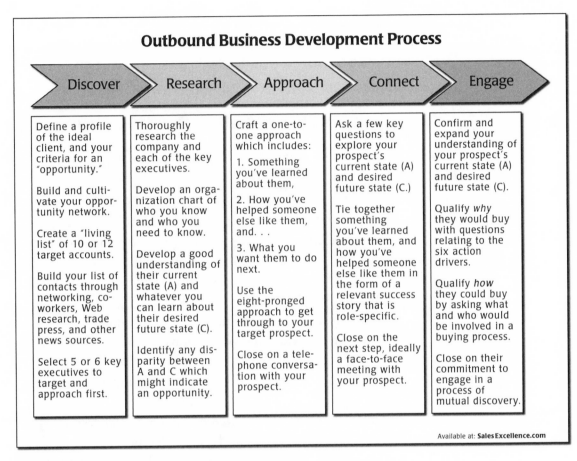

Figure 3.2 Outbound Business Development Process

The Research Stage

Always prepare before approaching your prospect, especially when approaching executives. Thoroughly research the company to build your knowledge of their current state (A). Also be on the lookout for any desired future state (C) that your prospective client might want to pursue. The company research template in Figure 3.3 on page 61 can be very helpful in assisting you to make sure you have a basic understanding of your customer's business before you begin your approach.

Some of the best resources for finding the information you need include:

1. *Company Web site:* Specifically the investor relations section.
2. *Annual report:* Especially the letter to the shareholders in the front.
3. *Securities and Exchange Commission (SEC) filings:* Form 10-K, Form 10-Q, or Form 8K for your publicly held prospects; these contain a tremendous amount of information about the company and their business model.
4. *Proxy statement:* Foreshadows the annual shareholders meeting of publicly held companies.
5. *Press releases:* Often announce new goals, initiatives, achievements, executive promotions, or mergers and acquisitions.
6. *News articles:* Often contain useful and informative quotes you can refer to in your approach.
7. *Analyst reports or recorded quarterly conference calls:* Can give you an in depth understanding of your prospect's goals and objectives as well as their plans to achieve them.

Reading through an annual report or a 10-K filing can be quite boring unless you are reading to learn something specific. Review the company research template before you begin researching each new client to remind yourself of what you are actually trying to learn. In addition to researching your prospect's company, also try to learn some things about each of the key executives that you intend to contact. The executive research template shown in Figure 3.4 is a great tool to help you get started.

Company Research Template

Business Model: How do they use their assets to serve their customers and make a profit for their shareholders (i.e., how do they make money)?

Market: What vertical industries, horizontal business functions, or customer segments are they focused on? Who are some of their key customers?

Business Strategies: What is their growth strategy (merger and acquisition vs. organic growth)? What is their investment strategy (infrastructure, technology, human capital)?

Market Position: How are they doing within the markets they are focused on (i.e., market share or market penetration)?

Go-To-Market Strategy: How do they position themselves in the marketplace? Do they have a unique competitive advantage in their market?

Competition: What other companies (or market forces) do they compete against consistently? Who are their primary competitors and how well do they compete?

Competitive Differentiation: What makes them different from their competitors in terms of their products and services, their company, or their people?

SWOT: What are their primary *strengths* and *weaknesses*? What do they perceive as their greatest *opportunities* or *threats*?

External Factors: What pending legislation, litigation, government regulations, or changing industry standards could impact their business?

Recent Performance: How have they done compared to their own historical performance, and compared to competitors (stock price, growth, profitability)?

Outlook for the Future: What do they believe the next few quarters or next few years will hold for them? What does the analyst community think?

Goals and Objectives: What are their stated business goals and objectives? Do they state any of the strategies or tactics they will employ to achieve them?

Available at: **Sales Excellence.com**

Figure 3.3 Company Research Template

Executive Research Template

Personal Background: Where did he or she grow up? Where did they go to college? Where do they live now? Do they have a family? What are their hobbies or personal interests?

Corporate Pedigree: Where did they work right out of college? Where else have they worked since then? Where did they work their longest stint? What has been their career path thus far? How long have they been in their current position?

Relationships and Alliances: Were they brought into their current position by someone in particular? With whom do they align themselves within their company? Who within (or outside) their company could influence their decisions?

Compensation and Incentives: How are they measured, evaluated, and compensated in their current position (salary, stock options, bonuses, etc.)?

Personal or Career Motives: What are their career plans and goals moving forward? How can you help them achieve those goals?

Available at: **SalesExcellence.com**

Figure 3.4 Executive Research Template

Begin to develop an organization chart that includes the people you currently know and whom you have researched. Also make note of who else you feel you need to meet so you can ask questions about them and seek opportunities to meet with them as you go along. Build your relationship footprint in each account as broadly as you can. This is covered in depth in Chapter Four.

Through your research, see if you can get an understanding of point A for each of the people whom you suspect may be involved in any future buying process. Also learn whatever you can about their most highly desired C. Ideally, you would identify one or more disparities between A and C that might indicate an opportunity and that you could refer to as you approach your prospect.

The Approach Stage

The approach stage is when you actually reach out to your target prospect. I recommend developing a carefully crafted and personalized approach for each individual on your target prospect list. Every time you attempt to reach them, regardless of the medium (letter, phone, voice mail, etc.), you should include the three essential elements of a successful approach, which are:

1. Something you've learned about them.
2. How you've helped someone else like them.
3. What you want them to do next.

Sharing something you've learned about them and how you've helped someone else like them demonstrates that you took the time to do your homework. This can be a powerful differentiator in itself. Even more importantly, you will be talking about something that matters to them instead of talking about yourself. When you mention the name of a client who had a similar problem, you build credibility and create curiosity.

The third element, which is sometimes called your call to action, is especially important. Always let your prospect know the next reasonable step if they'd like to learn more or move forward. They might not be willing to take the next step you want them to take, such as an introductory meeting with you, but if you don't ask, they surely won't. These three elements should be a part of every prospecting approach.

Leverage every form of communication to try to get through to your prospect. Using only one or two mediums can severely limit your chances of success. If all you do is leave voice mails or send out letters and wait for people to call you back, you'll be a very frustrated salesperson. If you just hammer out cold calls but haven't softened up your target prospect with some previous communication, those calls can be very awkward and unproductive.

Until you try, you'll never know which communication medium is going to work with any particular prospect. I suggest adopting a process that includes a wide variety of mediums to try to get through. In our workshops, we teach participants how to write introductory letters, how to be more effective on the phone, and how to use multiple forms of communication all combined into a process that I call the eight-pronged approach. This process includes these eight mediums:

1. *Letter:* Written specifically to the individual you are trying to reach (not a form letter), and including the three essential elements of a successful approach mentioned earlier.
2. *Fax:* Sent as a follow-up to your letter to request a scheduled time to speak with your prospect on the phone.
3. *Voice mail:* Includes a specific window of time when they can call you back and reach you in person.
4. *E-mail:* Sent just after you leave your voice mail letting your prospect know they can respond either way to schedule a time to speak on the phone.
5. *Written message:* Taken by your prospect's administrative assistant to be handed to your prospect or placed on their desk.
6. *Telephone call:* Placed between 7:00 and 8:30 a.m., during the lunch hour, or between 5:00 and 6:30 p.m. to reduce the chances of having your call screened by the administrative assistant.
7. *Notes, cards, etc.:* Any kind of unique or unusual written message that is different from the dozens of other things they receive in the mail each day.
8. *Drop by:* If you happen to be in the area. You may not be able to see the executive, but perhaps you could meet their assistant.

Eight-Pronged Approach Worksheet

Account: _Delcom Technologies_

Contacts:	Letter	Fax	Phone (Voice Mail)	E-Mail	Written Message	Phone (Voice Mail)	Note or Card	Drop By	First Meeting
Roger Smith, VP of Operations	Feb 21	Feb 27	Feb 28	Feb 28	Mar 1	Mar 2	———→		Mar 18
JoAnne Simpson, CFO	Feb 21	Feb 27	Feb 28	Feb 28		Mar 2	Mar 10		
Bob Anderson, VP of R&D	Feb 21	Feb 27	Feb 28	Feb 28					
Jennifer Connors, Controller	Feb 21	Feb 27	Mar 1	Mar 1	Mar 3	Mar 5	Mar 6	Mar 8	Mar 12
Daniel King, VP of Engineering	Feb 21	Feb 27	Mar 1	Mar 1		Mar 5	Mar 10		
Tim Turner, Dir. of Logistics	Feb 28	Mar 6	Mar 7	Mar 7		Mar 9			
Frank McLane, Engineering Mgr.	Feb 28	Mar 6	Mar 7	Mar 7			Mar 10		
Diane Patts, Engineering Mgr.	Mar 1	Mar 7	Mar 8	Mar 8	Mar 9	Mar 10	———→		Mar 14
Tom Wong, Design Engineer									
Bob Burns, Design Engineer									
Ron Sanders, Dir. of R&D	Mar 3	Mar 8	Mar 9	Mar 9					
Bob Cox, Dir. of Procurement	Mar 3	Mar 8	Mar 9				———→		Mar 12
Toni Ricardo, Procurement	Mar 3	Mar 8	Mar 9	Mar 9					

Available at: **SalesExcellence.com**

> The objective of the eight-pronged approach is to book a meeting with one or more people within your prospect's organization.

> By targeting and approaching several different people at once, you can accelerate your business development process and build your relationship footprint much more quickly.

> When you book an appointment to visit your client, make several additional calls to see who else you could possibly meet with while you are there.

Figure 3.5 Eight-Pronged Approach Worksheet

Any of these mediums on its own can be a good way to get through to your prospective customer. But when used together as a series of correspondence, they are incredibly effective. To track your progress and monitor where you are with each person you're approaching, you can use the eight-pronged approach worksheet shown in Figure 3.5.

This worksheet can be used to track the date that each step is taken with each of your target contacts within an account. This will help you keep track of the next step with each person you are approaching within your prospect's company. It will also help you be more consistent with your follow through and accelerate your business development process. The objective is to get a meeting with several different people within the account, if possible.

Of the key executives you've identified and researched, you have no way of knowing which ones will be responsive and which ones won't. To compress your business development process and cut time out of your sales cycle, I recommend approaching them all at once. This also reduces the likelihood of getting stuck selling to one person.

If the CRM (customer relationship management) or SFA (sales force automation) software your company uses can capture and manage this information—*and* if it is easy to access and update—that's great. But sometimes the best tool for the job is a pen and paper copy of this worksheet kept readily available in your binder or briefcase.

As you approach each person you've targeted, build and leverage a relationship with his or her administrative assistant. Assistants can become your greatest ally or your worst adversary depending on how you treat them. A good rule of thumb is, if you want to sell *past* the assistant, sell *to* the assistant. Treat them with the same respect you would treat their boss, and make the sale of why their boss should take the time to speak to you.

If the people you initially call on don't respond to your approach, reach out to some of the other people within the company. Knock on every door that you think is worth knocking on until you get through or you are convinced there is no opportunity. Then come back and knock on all of them again in a few months. Several of the people on the other side of the door might have changed or might simply be in a better mood that day. Once you get through to a prospect, close on a scheduled telephone conversation.

The Connect Stage

When you connect by phone, avoid broadcasting everything about yourself and your company. Try to start a conversation. You may have been told to prepare an "elevator pitch" to use either on the phone or in person. The idea is that if you got onto an elevator with a key executive, you would have a prepared pitch that you could broadcast to them during the 30 seconds it would take to get to their floor. I'd like to encourage you to forget about an elevator pitch! Instead, craft two or three good elevator questions that you can use in person or on the phone.

Make sure that your example of how you've helped someone else like them is role-specific. Don't call a finance executive and tell her all the technical details of how you helped the database administrator of some other company. Make sure that any success story you share relates to the position they occupy. Once you start a conversation, see if you can further explore their current state (A) and their desired future state (C). Seek to discover or confirm a disparity between where they are now and where they want to be.

Before you end the call, close on the next step. If you are an outside sales professional, this would ideally be a face-to-face meeting. If you sell primarily over the phone, this would be a scheduled call for the purpose of further mutual discovery.

The Engage Stage

The final stage of your BD process involves additional discovery at a face-to-face meeting or on a scheduled telephone call. This is where you will start qualifying the opportunity by learning why they would buy and how they could buy if they wanted to. If you feel there is a good opportunity that is worth investing your time in, you can engage with your client in a process of mutual discovery.

At this stage, the objective is to close on their commitment to arrange additional meetings with key personnel. This should include those who would be involved in evaluating or using what you sell, as well as those who would provide oversight for the associated project and approval for the investment.

Tracking Your Business Development Results

To maximize your success using your business development process, you can track your progress using the business development worksheet shown in Figure 3.6. This worksheet is designed to help you plan, measure, and manage your business development activity to maximize your results. It mirrors the five stages of the outbound business development process shown in Figure 3.2.

The business development worksheet lists your 10 or 12 target accounts and records the date on which you discovered, researched, approached, connected, met with, and engaged in a process of mutual discovery with each prospect. You can see exactly what you need to do next with each one. Tracking the date on which each step takes place—and how much time has passed since the last step was taken—helps you to stay focused and tends to accelerate your business development process, which leads to shorter sales cycles.

When you start tracking your business development success, you will discover your actual conversion rates for approaches, phone calls, and introductory meetings that you can use in future activity planning. Simply total the number of dates that appear in each column, and divide that number by the total in the previous column. You gain tremendous confidence when you prove to yourself that when you approach nine people, you'll have seven productive phone calls, five productive meetings, and find two new opportunities to add to your portfolio.

Your 30-Day Business Development Plan

Effective business development requires a commitment to doing some things that you'd probably rather not do. Very few sales professionals love prospecting, but the successful ones make it a habit and learn to focus on the results as opposed to the effort.

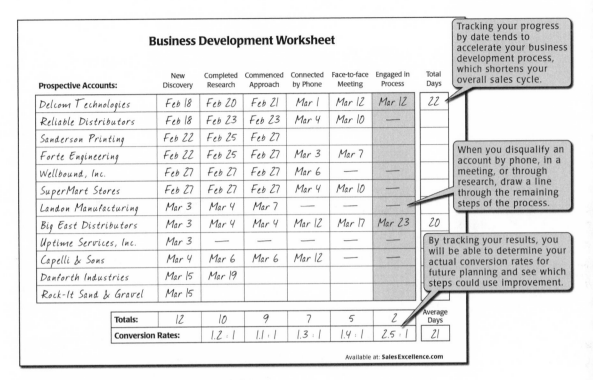

Figure 3.6 Business Development Worksheet

I know that you're not going to get excited about any program that asks you to commit a certain number of hours to prospecting every week for the rest of your life. Can you just make a commitment of what you are willing to do for the next 30 days? Guidelines for developing your own 30-day business development plan appear in Figure 3.7.

Create a prospecting plan of action that you can live with, execute your plan for the next 30 days, and then step back and evaluate how you did. Maybe you will decide to target some different roles or job titles next month. You might want to lead with a fax instead of a letter, tweak your voice mail message to evoke your prospect's curiosity, or craft a couple of key questions that can help you make the sale to the executive assistant and earn your way to their boss.

30-Day Business Development Plan

Step 1: Decide which companies you would most like to add to your opportunity portfolio and ultimately to your client list.

Step 2: Decide which executives within those accounts would most likely play a major role in any decision to buy what you sell.

Step 3: Decide which mediums of communication (letter, fax, telephone, voice mail, e-mail, etc.) you will use to get through.

Step 4: Decide which tools and templates you intend to employ. Organize yourself so that you can be productive during every prospecting minute.

Step 5: Decide how much time you will invest in business development on a daily or weekly basis. Plan and manage your time carefully.

Step 6: Execute relentlessly for the next 30 days. Don't let anything get in your way or knock you off track!

Available at: **SalesExcellence.com**

Figure 3.7. Your 30-Day Business Development Plan

The key is to work your plan for the next 30 days, evaluate your results, and adjust your plan accordingly. In this way, you will ensure that you are doing what is required to find new opportunities on a regular basis so you'll always have plenty of deals to work on. This will minimize the negative effects of the business development roller coaster.

* * *

Once you engage in a sales opportunity with a new client, you'll need to meet as many different people as you can within the account, qualify the opportunity with everyone you meet, and structure the opportunity to close. The next three chapters are designed to help you accomplish these three objectives.

CHAPTER FOUR

Navigating and Selling Your Way to the Executive Level

In today's business world, very few major decisions are made by a single person. If what you sell represents a substantial financial investment or a broad organizational impact for your customer, there will likely be a number of different approvers and influencers involved, not just one all-powerful "decision maker." Some of these buying roles will be played by senior-level executives. Therefore, learning how to navigate your customer's organization, engage executives in the buying process, and be effective selling at the executive level is vital to your success.

When it comes to selling to executives, there are two major issues that participants in my workshops always seem to be concerned with: (1) How do you get through to and secure an audience with a senior executive? and (2) Once you do get in front of the executive, what should you say or do?

In Chapter Three, we talk about outbound business development, how to target and research certain executives within a company, and how to leverage multiple forms of communication to initiate contact and gain access. Chapter Seven deals specifically with translating the capabilities of your products and services into financial results so you'll be more effective once you finally do get in front of the executive. In this chapter, we focus on navigating your customer's organization and earning access to executive-level approvers and influencers by working your way up from the bottom.

We begin by considering why we should be selling to executives in the first place and by looking at the various roles that an executive might play in our customer's buying process. Then we explore the various strategies and techniques for earning our way past gatekeepers so we can sell both higher and wider within our customer's organization.

Why Sell at the Executive Level?

As I work with salespeople from all over the world, I see the same deficiency in an alarmingly high percentage of opportunities: We don't know enough people within our customer's organization. In most cases it's not that we are selling to the wrong people; it's that we are not selling to enough of the right people in each account.

When I reflect back on sales opportunities that I lost, I often think, "I wish I had insisted on meeting the VP of engineering *before* I presented my final proposal to the CFO. That would have changed my entire strategy." Or, "If I had known the VP of marketing had so much influence, I would have taken the time to get to know her much better." Meeting more people, and especially the executives involved in those deals, would have enabled me to learn more. Had I known more, I might have done things differently.

Meeting the executives that play a role in our customer's buying decision gives us much greater perspective on why they would buy. We can understand the executive's perception of their current state (A), their desired future state (C), their motive and urgency, as well as the associated consequences and risks. It also enables us to get a more complete understanding of all the steps they would need to take before they would be able to buy.

Conversely, if we don't learn to sell beyond Clem and engage the executives who will make the larger decisions, we may never understand the context of the buying decision (which we talk about in Chapter Two), whether there is an executive predisposition to one of the vendors being considered, or what other projects and/or initiatives we are really competing with. If we don't get the viewpoints and opinions of the various people who will be involved in the buying process, we can't properly position ourselves to win the opportunity, or qualify whether there is even an opportunity to win.

Selling to only one or two people in an account is incredibly risky. No matter how forthcoming they are or how much they like us and our product, we never really get the whole picture. We can't craft an effective strategy if we have only one person's opinion. What's worse, if that person suddenly leaves, retires, transfers, or gets fired, then we are in big trouble.

How high do you need to sell? That depends. You should sell as high as you need to in order to close the deal. In a small company, that could be the president who also happens to be the owner. In a large corporation, a vice president of engineering could provide approval for the project. But you might have to work with the controller to get the funds released and the head of procurement to obtain the purchase order. What determines how high you need to sell is an understanding of who will play the key roles in your customer's overall buying decision.

The Roles Involved in a Buying Decision

There is no way to know exactly how many people we will need to meet in order to ensure your success in each account. But in some of the opportunities in your portfolio, it's probably safe to say that you should know more people than you know right now. Of all the people who will play a significant buying role in your best sales opportunity, which ones are you *not* selling to currently? Let's do a short exercise to find out.

Who Do You Know?

Select what you consider to be your best prospective opportunity from your current opportunity portfolio (pipeline). Think about who you currently know within your prospective client's organization.

Take a blank sheet of paper and draw a small rectangle near the middle. In that box, write the name and title of your primary contact—the person you most frequently talk with or who you know best. Also, make note of the role you think he or she might play in the overall buying process.

From there, begin to construct what I call a buying roles chart—like the one in Figure 4.1—by adding more rectangles that will contain the names, titles, and roles of the other contacts that you know within that account. These could be the superiors, subordinates, or coworkers of your primary contact or anyone else you have met even if you're not sure where they fit in the organization. Once you have determined who you know, let's talk about who you don't know.

Who Do You Need to Meet?

Add to your buying roles chart by identifying any other people you have heard of—who you think might play a significant role in your customer's buying process—but you have *not* actually spoken to yet.

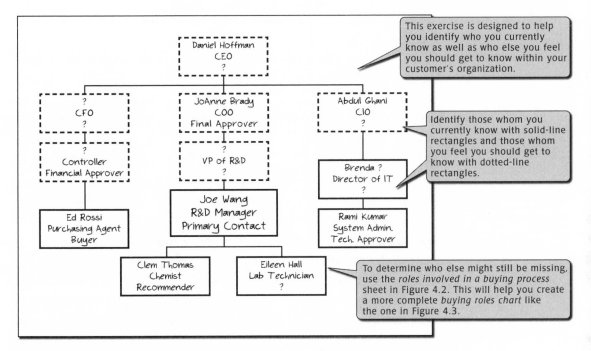

Figure 4.1 Buying Roles Exercise

For these people, draw rectangles made from dotted lines. If you don't know each person's full name at this point, at least identify them by title or role if you can.

At this point, your buying roles chart might look something like the example in Figure 4.1. Now, let's take our exercise to the next level by looking at all the various roles that might be involved in a complex buying process.

The Roles Involved in a Buying Process

If it's true that we need to meet more people within each prospective account, the question is, "Who else do we need to meet?" To help answer this question, please take a look at roles involved in a buying process in Figure 4.2.

Using this list as a reference, look at the buying roles chart you've begun and identify who would likely play each of these roles in your prospect's buying process. Any individual could play more than one role, but don't assume that the "big boss" will play them all. Companies use a consensus approach to decision making much more than they did five or ten years ago. The specific roles involved in the decision to buy the products or services that you sell could be different from these, but this should provide a good start. Let's look closely at each type.

Recommenders. One very common role in a buying process is the recommender. This is Clem or a selection committee that acts as a collective Clem. In a top-down opportunity, recommenders are charged by an executive to explore the purchase decision (which we discuss in Chapter Two) and recommend the best product or services solution and the best source to provide it.

In a bottom-up opportunity, however, recommenders can spend a lot of time looking for just the right solution and source *before* they go to upper management to see if there is any need or interest. This is why it is so important for us to get beyond the recommenders as early as possible and meet some of the other players involved.

Owners. When selling big-ticket items in a complex selling environment, we need to sell high enough to find the person who has the authority to invest and the responsibility to earn. I call this the investment owner. This is the person who is responsible for earning a profit on the money that they invest in your solutions.

We also need to find the person who will oversee and own the project or initiative that the purchase of our products and services is tied to. I call this the project owner. Until your customer has identified who will accept the responsibility of these two roles, they

Roles Involved in a Buying Process

Recommender(s)
Person or committee who provides a recommendation of what to buy and who to buy it from.

Project Owner
Ultimately responsible for the successful completion of the project associated with the purchase of your solution.

Investment Owner
Ultimately responsible for earning the promised return on the investment in your solution.

Corporate Influencer/Approver
Influences the buying decision from a *corporate approval* standpoint.

Policy Influencer
Influences the buying decision from a *company policy* standpoint.

Political Influencer
Anyone who stands to gain or lose politically based on the outcome of the buying decision.

Consultant Influencer
Consultant from outside the company who can influence the buying decision.

"Old Dog" Influencer
Influencial simply because he or she has "been around forever."

Solution Approver
Answers the question: Will this solution do the job we need it to do and help us accomplish our desired result?

Technical Approver
Answers the question: Will this solution work with our current systems, processes, and infrastructure?

Staffing/Implementation Plan Approver
Approves the plan to implement and use your solution as well as staff the associated project.

Financial Approver
Provides approval to release funds for budgeted expenditures or to allocate or obtain funding for capital investments.

Legal/Contract Approver
Provides legal approval for the terms and conditions of your contract or agreement.

Final Approver
Gives final approval for the buyer to release the purchase order or the contract signer to sign the contract.

Buyer/Contract Signer
The person who actually issues the purchase order or signs the contract.

Available at: **SalesExcellence.com**

Figure 4.2 The Roles Involved in a Buying Process

probably won't buy anything. Trying to win an opportunity without meeting and qualifying the people who will own the success of the project and the return on investment could ultimately prove to be a complete waste of your time and effort.

Influencers. There are a number of different kinds of influencers involved in most complex buying decisions. If you're selling to one division (or a subsidiary) of a larger company, there will probably be influencers at Corporate who have a say in any major decision. There are also policy influencers, such as a global sourcing group, that will allow purchases only from preapproved vendors.

There could be one or more outside consultants who have been hired specifically for their opinions and advice on a given project. The buying process could also be influenced by anyone in the company who stands to gain or lose politically by an investment in your solutions. And don't forget about Fred—who I call the *old dog* influencer—who has been at the company for 29 years and won't accept a promotion, but who seems to have a say in every major buying decision.

Approvers. Any substantial buying decision will require sign-off from one or more approvers. Buying your products and services could require someone to provide approval for:

- The viability of your solution to actually help them get to point C on time and on budget.
- The technical specifications and requirements of your solution.
- Prioritizing the project or initiative that your solution is tied to.
- The funding for the purchase and the project that it is tied to.
- The staffing resources that will be needed and the implementation plan to put your solution to use.
- The terms and conditions of your contract or license agreement.

Also, the person who will ultimately issue the purchase order or sign your contract normally needs to get final approval from someone else before they can place the order. Depending on the size of the transaction, you might need the cooperation of a dozen people to close the deal.

*　*　*

After working through this exercise, most of the participants in my workshops identify one or more key players in their customer's buying process who they don't yet know. For some people, this is a major wake-up call revealing serious deficiencies in their knowledge of who they will need to work with to bring the opportunity to closure. If this has happened to you, at least now you realize that you have work to do, and you have a much better idea of who else you need to be selling to.

Whether the buying roles chart you drew is reasonably complete—or is full of gaping holes—let me remind you that we did this exercise using your very best prospect. The question is, "How well do you know the approvers and influencers in opportunities 2 through 12 in your portfolio?"

Completing Your Buying Roles Chart

I recommend creating a buying roles chart like the one in Figure 4.3 on page 81 for every opportunity on your sales forecast and for every significant opportunity in your pipeline. Identify each person who will be involved in your customer's buying process by name, title, and role. If possible, arrange to meet all the people who you think will be involved in bringing the opportunity to closure.

Any opportunity that you feel is worth investing your time in is also worth the time it will take to develop a complete buying roles chart. This will help you track your progress as you grow your relationship footprint within each account.

Two Major Strategies for Selling Higher

There are two major strategies for selling higher and wider within your customer's company. One strategy is to engage high and sell your way down through your client's organization (top-down). The other approach is to engage low and sell your way up (bottom-up). While some opportunities or accounts are perfectly suited to selling top-down, many will require that you also sell bottom-up. To be successful, you will need to become familiar with and effective in using both strategies.

Engaging High

One key strategy for selling higher within your customer's organization is to start high to begin with. This involves using the outbound business development techniques we discuss in Chapter Three so that you reach out to your prospective customer *before* they contact you.

This is definitely a time-consuming and labor-intensive approach. It requires a great deal of stamina and a thick skin because many of the organizations you approach won't recognize a need for what you sell. Others will have a previous relationship with a different vendor who you won't be able to displace.

This approach should be part of your overall game plan for your territory. Identify the companies that you have never sold to but that you believe could become excellent customers, and call them before they get a chance to call you. Also consider targeting a few companies that are known strongholds for your competitors. You might be surprised to discover that not everyone within that company is happy working with their current vendor. There are probably many gaps

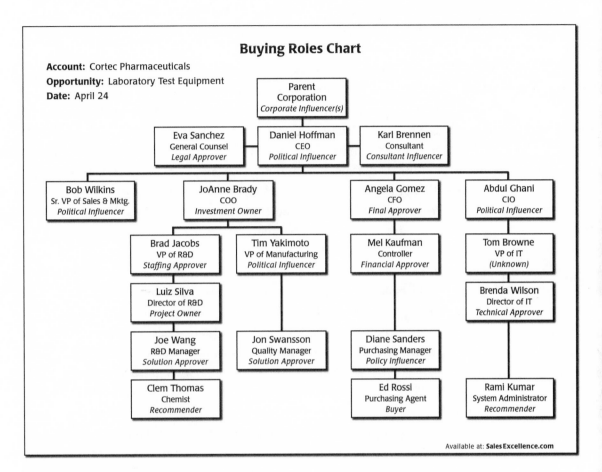

Figure 4.3 Buying Roles Chart

between where your prospective client is now and where they would really like to be.

Using the outbound business development process, introduce yourself to several key people at the executive level. In some cases, you will discover or create a new opportunity. Even if you don't, you will at least have established a contact that you can reach out to again if you happen to receive a lead from someone else in that company in the future.

Engaging Low

When a prospective client contacts us, we usually have to start at the bottom of the organization and work our way up. Ironically, this often happens in the late stages of a top-down opportunity—where Clem is tasked with researching and selecting a vendor and a solution to be used as part of a project that is already approved and funded.

One of the most common questions I hear in sales workshops is, "What if you've started working with Clem, but you know you need to be selling higher in the organization? What do you do?" Well, there are only three things that you can do:

1. Just Sell to Clem. One way to proceed would be to sell only to Clem and let him interface with everyone else within his company. This is a very high-risk approach. First of all, unless we can talk to the other people involved in the buying process to understand their perception of point C, we will never know how to properly position our B. We end up shooting in the dark and hoping they like whatever we happen to propose.

With this approach we will also never be able to understand who and what would be involved in their overall buying process. The best we can do is jump through whatever hoops Clem asks us to jump through and keep our fingers crossed. Under most circumstances, this is not a viable strategy.

2. Go over Clem's Head and Call the Big Boss. Another way to handle this situation would be to go over Clem's head and call his boss or someone higher up in the company. As tempting as this approach is, it is probably even more risky than the first one. In many situations, Clem will be the primary user or the administrator of whatever solution you sell to his company. Rarely can you win without Clem's recommendation. To ignore Clem, or disrespect him by blatantly going over his head, will probably hurt you more than it will help.

3. Earn Your Way to Higher Levels within the Company. The most effective strategy for selling higher once you've already engaged is to earn your way past Clem to higher levels within your prospect's company. To do this, you have to understand why Clem is so resistant to the idea in the first place and then learn what to say or do to help him change his mind.

* * *

Of these three approaches, the third is the only good long-term solution. Learning to sell your way up from the bottom is one of the most valuable skills you can develop.

Earning Your Way Past the Gatekeeper

There are two different kinds of gatekeepers we encounter within an organization. One is the executive assistant, who we talk about in Chapter Three. The other kind of gatekeeper is someone like Clem—who is an individual contributor or a frontline manager. To earn your way past Clem, it's important to understand the psychology of why a gatekeeper is a gatekeeper.

The Psychology of a Gatekeeper

In a top-down opportunity, Clem is asked to engage a number of vendors in an evaluation and selection process. Clem screens us from talking to his superiors because he feels it is his responsibility to do so. If we go over his head, it makes it look like he wasn't doing his job.

In a bottom-up opportunity, Clem starts evaluating products and services and when he finds one he thinks his company needs, then he goes to management to see if he can get the funding and approval to buy it. In this case, if Clem's management were to find out he was watching product demonstrations instead of working on all the other projects on his plate, that wouldn't look very good.

We need to quickly determine which of these two scenarios we are dealing with. Then we have to figure out some way to make Clem look good so he will want to take us to his boss. Later in this chapter, I share several proven techniques to accomplish this.

The Psychology of Getting Past the Gatekeeper

There is a certain mindset that is a critical part of selling beyond the gatekeeper. Our objective should be to get past Clem and on to some of the other people involved in the buying decision within the first three meetings or three extended telephone calls. If we don't get past Clem within the first three meetings, we probably never will. A precedent is established that can be very difficult to overcome.

In my workshops, I often joke about how this relationship with Clem is somewhat like dating. When you meet with Clem, make it clear—through your words and your actions—that you are not ready to settle down just yet. You're meeting with other people at his company, too. Ideally, you will have a few other meetings or telephone calls with some of the other people in the company either scheduled or already completed. This way Clem doesn't get the idea that the relationship is exclusive.

On the other hand, if you meet with Clem three, four, or five times—and never hint that you want to meet with other people— Clem starts thinking that all your attention and free lunches are reserved for him. If you court Clem exclusively for two or three months and then decide to call someone else without telling him, it's no wonder he gets upset. He feels jilted!

Make every effort to continue to meet and talk to more people within your client's organization every time you visit. Constantly be looking for ways to grow your relationship footprint. Don't ignore Clem; treat him with all the respect you can. But sell to the other influencers and approvers as well. *Don't marry Clem!*

Eight Techniques for Selling Higher and Wider

Every big sale is just a series of little sales. One of the most important little sales you can make is selling Clem on why he should *want you* to talk to some of the other people in his company. Help him make whatever internal sale he needs to make and help him look good in the process. The following are eight techniques that will help you make the sale of why you should meet with more of the people involved.

1. Use the Customer Results Model with Your Clients

When you focus on your customer's desired outcomes and results, as opposed to the products that you sell, your customer starts to think of you less as a salesperson and more like a partner. Many of my clients find it helpful to use the customer results model (the ABC diagram from Chapter Two) in conversations with their customers.

Go up to a whiteboard or flipchart and draw out ABC. Start the conversation like this:

Today, we are here at what we call point A. We would like to learn as much about your current state as you are comfortable sharing with us. But we also want to spend some time exploring what we call point C.

That's your desired future state. If we can get a good understanding of some of the major projects that are underway or where you want to take your business over the next two to five years, then we'll see if we have a solution—a B—that can help you get there. Does that sound fair?

You will need to practice this a few times and use your own words to sell the idea, but when your prospective customer sees that you are there to understand and help them instead of push your product, you will get a very positive response. This will naturally lead to conversations with other people within their company because the discussion is focused on your client's business and not on the products that you sell. When you turn the meeting into an interactive discussion about their desired business results, don't be surprised when someone in the room says, "Can you hold on for just a minute? I'd like to get my boss in here to hear this."

2. Ask about the Context of the Buying Decision

When you focus on your customer's C and ask questions about their desired results and the goals they are trying to accomplish, you help Clem realize the importance of the context of the buying decision. Some good questions would include:

- What is the ultimate goal you are trying to accomplish?
- What is your strategy or your plan to achieve it?
- Is there a certain project underway that this solution would be a part of?
- How will you justify and account for the investment?
- How does this particular project fit into your overall business strategy?

One of the reasons that a gatekeeper doesn't want you to meet their boss is that they are afraid you will just broadcast the same message to their boss that you broadcasted to them. When Clem sees that you are not there to just read a list of features and benefits, he will begin to feel that you are worthy of talking to his boss.

3. Craft and Use Access Questions

One way to help Clem understand why we need to meet other people is to ask specific questions that he doesn't know the answer to. I call these access questions. At my company, Sales Excellence, we receive a lot of calls from marketing or human resource personnel who are trying to gather information about sales training. We start by listening to everything they are willing to tell us about their company and their selling environment.

When the time feels right, we ask, "If you did put together a workshop for your sales team, what would you want the participants to be thinking or doing the day after the workshop that would be different from what they were thinking or doing the day before? What are the observable changes in sales behavior you would like to see?"

In many cases, the immediate response is, "Actually, I'm calling on behalf of our vice president of sales. Perhaps we'd better get him involved." The question is designed to cause that reaction and to earn access to the executive.

If the first question doesn't work, we ask another access question, such as: "What are the measures—besides just sales revenue—that you currently use to gauge the effectiveness of your sales team that we could use as a metric to measure the ongoing impact of this training?" If the first access question doesn't help us get through to management, the second one usually does.

You will have to craft your own access questions that fit your industry and your specific selling situation. Questions that relate directly to your customer's point C and the context of their buying decision work best. Hopefully, Clem will realize that he doesn't know the answer, and he will think it's a good idea for you to meet some of the other people in the company who do.

4. Sell across the Organization

Another great way to sell higher is to focus on selling wider. Gatekeepers are usually far more protective of their own boss than they are of the other executives in the company. As you develop your buying roles chart, identify the other people within your customer's organization who may play key roles in a buying decision and then come up with a good reason to contact them.

Ask Clem a few questions about how the problems his company is facing in his department are affecting other departments across the organization. See if there is any cross-organizational impact on the sales department by using questions such as:

- How does this problem with product quality impact your vice president of sales?
- Is the sales department experiencing an increase in product returns?
- What effect is that having on customer satisfaction and customer retention?
- Are sales numbers suffering as a result?

Or ask questions about the impact on the finance department such as:

- How does this quality problem affect your CFO?
- Is your accounts receivable department having problems with collections?
- What kind of impact is this having on cash flow and profitability?

If Clem doesn't know the answers to these questions, ask him, "What do you think is the best way for us to find out?"

5. Bring Someone with You to Your Meeting

One way to justify why Clem should invite his boss to your next meeting is by bringing your boss, or someone else who can add value to the discussion. Decide who within your customer's organization you need to meet and then bring along someone from your company in a similar role.

If your company has technical experts who conduct product demonstrations and know your product line inside-out, bring them to meet some of the technical experts in your client's company. If you want to meet your customer's controller, then bring along someone from your company who can talk about return on investment and financing options. Don't expect Clem to invite his COO to meet your technical expert. That would be a mismatch. Use the appropriate people on your side to help you earn access to the right people on their side.

6. Trade Something They Want for the Access You Want

When Clem asks you to do a product demo, you could respond by asking, "If we did prepare a product demonstration, would you mind if I interviewed each of the people who will attend before the presentation?"

Or if Clem asks you for a proposal, you could say, "Suppose we were willing to prepare a proposal. Would you introduce me to the people who would be responsible for reviewing it and approving it so we could make sure it hits the bull's-eye?"

Notice that these questions are posed in a hypothetical fashion. You are actually negotiating with your customer by trading something they want for something you want. We explore this technique much further in Chapter Nine.

Sometimes your prospect thinks they only need a few things from you: a product demonstration, a proposal with your best price, and three references. The key is to determine exactly what you want in terms of access and information so you can trade it for the things your prospective client wants from you. Make sure you get all the access and information that you need before you run out of things to trade.

7. Create and Use a Customer Results Plan

In Chapter Six, we explore the use of a tool I call a customer results plan. This is, in essence, a project plan that defines all the things that you and your customer will work through together to get from point A (where they are now), to point C (where they want to be).

This is a phenomenal tool for gaining executive access, not only because it emphasizes your interest in partnering with your client, but because it spells out exactly who should be involved in the process from your own company and from your client's organization. When used properly, this is a fabulous way to justify why it's so important to get the key executives from your customer's company involved in certain steps in the overall buying process.

8. Create and Use a Customer Results Map

In Chapter Seven, we talk about a very powerful selling tool which I call a customer results map. Basically, it is a depiction of the various business strategies and tactical initiatives that your customer is using to pursue their goals and objectives.

You can create and use a customer results map as a way to link the capabilities of your products and services to the achievement of your customer's goals. It is extremely effective, especially in executive presentations and in persuading gatekeepers that their executive management might like to see how you've connected the dots between your solutions and their desired business results.

Those of you who have attended one of my workshops or have read *Think Like Your Customer* will recognize the customer results map as an extension of the Business Value Hierarchy™ concept. I have included a sample customer results map for eight different industries in the appendix.

* * *

These are just a few of the techniques you can use to sell beyond the gatekeeper and reach the executive level. In Chapter Seven, we go much deeper into how to be effective once you do earn access and get in front of a senior-level executive. But first, let's move on to Chapter Five, where we explore how we can leverage the relationships we've built to better qualify sales opportunities.

Qualifying Sales Opportunities with the Opportunity Scorecard

As a sales professional, your time is your most precious resource. Time is the currency with which you purchase your success, so to maximize your sales results, you'll have to spend it well. The key is deciding where to invest your time by choosing which prospects and sales opportunities offer the greatest potential return with the least downside risk. This is accomplished through sales qualification.

The purpose of qualifying sales opportunities is to determine the quality or "close-ability" of each deal. When done well, qualification enables us to better prioritize our efforts, craft sales strategy, more accurately forecast revenue, and properly allocate sales resources. Investing in the most highly qualified opportunities allows us to leverage our time and effort to maximize our selling results.

Qualifying sales opportunities is not simply a step in our process that is checked off as a yes or a no. It is an integral part of the ongoing process itself. You could even say it *is* the process. Thoroughly qualifying an opportunity usually takes multiple interactions with your customer, preferably with multiple people. And as conditions change throughout a sales cycle, an opportunity can be qualified one day and not qualified the next.

Determining the quality of sales opportunities requires that we understand how our customers think, how they make decisions, and what drives their buying behavior. What we really need to understand about each opportunity is why they would buy and how they could buy if they wanted to.

In this chapter, we explore the use of a powerful qualification tool which I call the opportunity scorecard. We discuss the principles on which it is based, as well as the various criteria we use to evaluate the quality or probability of sales opportunities. We talk about how to use the scorecard to qualify each deal in your sales portfolio and how to use what you learn to channel your sales efforts in order to maximize the potential of each opportunity.

The Opportunity Scorecard

The opportunity scorecard, as shown in Figure 5.1, is one of the most valuable tools of the results-based selling method. It is an evaluation tool based on a specific set of criteria which can be used to qualify every potential sales opportunity.

The opportunity scorecard serves several important purposes:

1. It provides a set of standard criteria for evaluating each opportunity, which enables a systematic approach to sales qualification.
2. It helps sales professionals determine the likelihood of each opportunity to ultimately come to closure so they can more easily prioritize the investment of their time and effort.
3. It illuminates the strengths and weaknesses of each sales opportunity, which enables sales professionals to craft better sales strategies, and it guides their efforts to improve the quality or probability of every deal.

Opportunity Scorecard   Date: _____

Account: _____   Opportunity: _____

Why would they buy?	Score each 0 to 5	How could they buy?	Score each 0 to 5
1. Current State (A)	—	11. Ownership/Oversight	—
2. Desired Future State (C)	—	12. Project Prioritization	—
3. Motive	—	13. Organizational Alignment	—
4. Urgency	—	14. Staffing/Implementation Plan	—
5. Payback/Return	—	15. Financial Approval	—
6. Means/Resources	—	16. Solution Approval	—
7. Consequence(s)	—	17. Legal/Contract Approval	—
8. Risk(s)	—	18. Vendor Recommendation	—
9. Solution Fit (B)	—	19. Final Approval	—
10. Relationships	—	20. Purchase/Agreement	—

Why Subtotal: _____

How Subtotal: _____

Total Probability out of 100: _____

Available at: **SalesExcellence.com**

> Using specific criteria to evaluate opportunities provides a systematic process for qualification, which leads to more accurate sales forecasts.

> The scorecard provides a common language for salespeople and their managers to talk about sales opportunities.

> More accurate sales qualification enables salespeople to better prioritize their time and effort in order to maximize their sales results.

Figure 5.1 The Opportunity Scorecard

4. It offers a method of measuring the probability of sales opportunities, which leads to higher success rates and more accurate sales forecasts.
5. It gives sales managers a common language with which to strategize and talk about sales opportunities with the salespeople on their team.

The opportunity scorecard is made up of a total of 20 different criteria on which to evaluate any sales opportunity. Ten criteria relate specifically to *why* customers buy, and ten relate to *how* customers buy.

Each of the criteria is used to score the sales opportunity on a scale of 0 to 5 (zero to five). When added together, they produce a total score out of a possible 100 that represents an estimate of the probability that the opportunity will ultimately come to closure.

This is not an exact science. We all know that situations and circumstances can change that would cause a very probable opportunity to stall temporarily or be derailed altogether. We also know that a score of zero on urgency, financial approval, or almost any other criteria can completely offset a high overall score. However, the accuracy of estimating probability with this approach far exceeds that of systems that gauge probability based on the stages of our sales process.

What makes the opportunity scorecard even more valuable is using it as an instrument to guide and focus our sales activity. If we score any particular opportunity and conclude that it is weak on motive, final approval, or any other criteria, this helps us focus our sales efforts in terms of who we meet with, the types of questions that we ask, and the selling that we do moving forward.

We can use the scorecard to quickly evaluate an opportunity before each interaction with our client. This provides guidance and structure for planning what we want to accomplish during the next meeting or telephone call. We can then revisit the scorecard afterward to measure our progress.

Qualifying Why Customers Buy

Effective qualification of a complex buying process goes far beyond the question of, "How many do they want to buy, and when do they want to buy them?" That question might be fine in a transactional selling environment where inbound leads find you and where the most you have to lose is a few minutes of your time on the phone.

But in a more complicated selling situation—with long sales cycles involving multiple influencers and approvers—this hardly scratches the surface of what we really need to know.

We need to understand *why* the customer would buy in the first place by examining the factors that drive our customer to take action to leave point A and move toward point C. The 10 elements of why customers buy are:

1. Current State (A)
2. Desired Future State (C)
3. Motive
4. Urgency
5. Payback/Return
6. Means/Resources
7. Consequence(s)
8. Risk(s)
9. Solution Fit (B)
10. Relationships

You will probably recognize many of these factors from Chapter Two. Numbers 3 through 8 are, of course, the action drivers, which play an extremely important role in your customers' buying decisions. Let's look at each of these 10 more closely.

1. Current State (A)

A vital part of building strong customer relationships is understanding your customer's business. Many customers will not feel comfortable doing business with a salesperson or a company that doesn't understand their industry, their market, and the specific business challenges they face.

As we discuss in Chapter Three, we should take the time to do some research on each significant sales opportunity. We should learn all we can about what they do, who they sell to, and who they compete with. We can accomplish some of this by reading the material they post on their Web site. But not everything that appears in a highly-polished press release or annual report is the real story from the inside.

When you get in front of your customer, ask questions that help you understand their perspective on the world. These questions don't have to be complicated. Your objective is to start a conversation so you can ask more questions. You could start with:

- How are things going, Mr. Thompson?
- What impact has the recent merger had on your department?
- How have the recent changes in regulatory compliance affected you?
- I read about your expansion plans in last year's annual report. How has that been going?

What you are looking for is a situation that your customer wants to change. The idea is to lead the conversation in the direction of a *disparity* between where they are now and where they would like to be in the future. The less comfortable your customer is with their current state, the more likely they are to buy what they need to change it.

2. Desired Future State (C)

Using the results-based selling method, it is essential to clearly understand what business results your customer is trying to accomplish so you can properly position your product or service as a viable solution. Ultimately, you want to paint the picture of a better future that they can create using your product and services or partnering with your company.

To get your customer talking about their desired point C, you can use transitional questions, such as:

- Sounds like things are going great. What are your plans going forward?
- That's a very aggressive goal. How do you plan to accomplish it?
- I'm sorry to hear about these problems. How do you envision them being solved?
- In a perfect world, how would this situation be different?

The key is to get your customer talking about how their current state could be improved and what their desired future state would look like.

One of the most versatile and effective questioning techniques for exploring point C is what I call the hypothetical question. Customers use this technique all the time. They say, "Suppose we decided to place the order today. When could we expect delivery?" Or, "If we wanted to move forward, would you be able to provide us with references?" What makes the hypothetical question so powerful is that it enables your customer to explore the possibilities of moving forward without committing to anything.

Using this technique to explore point C involves asking a three-part question. These three parts are designed to:

1. Set up the hypothetical.
2. Explore the possibilities.
3. Query for interest.

Take a look at the examples of all three parts in Figure 5.2 on page 101.

When you string all three parts together, your question will sound like one of these:

- What if you were able to eliminate the need for _____. Would that have an impact?
- Suppose you could reduce the occurrence of _____. Would that be worth looking into?

I encourage you to use these sample phrases in every conceivable combination and make up more of your own. The hypothetical question is very powerful because it is nonthreatening. It has broad application and can be used in a wide variety of ways which we explore throughout this book.

Your customer's point C could be as grandiose as increasing gross profit from 24 to 32 percent by using your software. It could also be as simple as switching to a vendor who can guarantee on-time delivery of subcomponents so they can be sure to meet their own delivery schedules. The more desirable their imagined future state, the more likely they will be to take action to get there.

3. Motive

As we discuss in Chapter Two, one of the conditions (action drivers) that drives your customer to take action to leave point A and venture out in pursuit of point C is their motive to get there. As we qualify sales opportunities, we should continually be asking ourselves, "Why would this company buy what I sell?" If we can't come up with a pretty good reason, they probably won't either.

Understanding your customer's motive is accomplished by asking them questions that begin with "Why...?" such as, "Why is this project such a high priority right now?" or, "Why does this disparity you've discovered constitute a problem?" We need to understand the context of the buying decision and what larger projects, plans, or

Hypothetical Questions to Explore Poi

Set Up the Hypothetical	Explore the Possibilities	Query for Interest
If you could . . .	solve the problem of . . .	Would that be good?
If it were possible that you could . . .	increase the efficiency of . . .	Would that help you?
What if you were able to . . .	accomplish the objective of . . .	Would that be useful?
Suppose you could . . .	improve your abilty to . . .	Would you like that?
Imagine that you were able to . . .	overcome the challenge of . . .	Would that have merit?
Assume, for a minute, that you could . . .	achieve the goal of . . .	Would that be significant?
Perhaps you could . . .	eliminate the need for . . .	Would that have an impact?
Envision yourself with the ability to . . .	improve the results of . . .	Would that improve matters?
Picture yourself being able to . . .	avoid the hassle of . . .	Would that make things better?
Visualize with me that you could . . .	increase the chances of . . .	Would that be valuable to you?
Consider the possibility you could . . .	reduce the time involved in . . .	Would that be of interest to you?
Let's suppose you had the ability to . . .	increase the likelihood that . . .	Would that be important to you?
Let's imagine that you were able to . . .	reduce the occurrence of . . .	Would that improve the situation?
Let's ponder the idea that you could . . .	eliminate the possibility of . . .	Would that be worth looking into?

Available at: **SalesExcellence.com**

Figure 5.2 Hypothetical Questions to Explore Point C

goals would motivate them to make a purchase so we can properly qualify the opportunity.

4. Urgency

One of the most important action drivers that moves your client to buy is their urgency to get to point C in a certain time frame. To gauge your customer's urgency, ask questions that begin with, "When...?" such as, "When do you need to have this project completed?" or, "When do you need to have this problem solved?"

If your customer doesn't have much of an urgency to move forward with a purchase, it is often because they have not clearly defined a C that offers enough of a payback or return to justify the investment of scarce resources and incur the associated risk. Until you find someone within your client's business who has some sort of urgency to reach point C, a buying decision can easily drag on from one month to the next, one quarter to the next, and even one year to the next, forever. This makes urgency one of the most important elements of qualifying why your customer would buy.

5. Payback/Return

Another major factor that affects your customer's willingness to invest in your solutions is the potential payback or return on their investment. If your customer believes that they stand to earn a substantial profit from their investment in your solutions, then they are obviously more likely to buy.

Asking questions that begin with, "How much...?" or, "How many...?" helps your customer to quantify payback or return. Some good questions could include, "How much faster could you get this product to market if we could cut your product test cycles in half?" Or, "How many hours could you save each month if you had to service these machines only once a week instead of every day?" Questions like these help you qualify whether your customer really understands and appreciates the potential return, not just the investment.

6. Means/Resources

No matter how strong their motive or their urgency, your customer can't buy if they don't have the money. Your customer must have the means and resources to buy *and use* whatever you sell them in order to reach their desired business results. It takes time, money, and human resources to get from A to C. We need to know if they can afford to make the trip.

To qualify your customer for means and resources, ask questions that begin with, "How would you...?" or, "What would be involved...?" Here are two examples: "How would you go about staffing a project of this magnitude?" Or, "What would be involved in getting funding for something like this?" The quality of your sales opportunity is strongly influenced by your customer's ability to make the needed resources available.

7. Consequence(s)

Even a customer who has a vision of a magnificent point C and has a strong motive to get there will usually put off buying until they absolutely have to. As part of our qualification process, we should always look for a consequence that would drive our customer to take action within a certain time frame.

Questions that utilize the phrase, "What if you don't...?" can be very helpful for this purpose. One example would be, "What if you don't do something to correct this problem right away?" You can also help your customer quantify the consequence by asking, "How much will this problem cost you each month if you don't do something about it?" It is imperative that we learn to ask questions about consequence in order to better qualify opportunities and improve forecast accuracy. The lack of a consequence for inaction is one of the most common reasons that customers delay or forgo a purchase altogether.

8. Risk(s)

Excessive risk is another common reason why customers *don't* buy. As I mention in Chapter Two, it doesn't matter if it's real or imagined. If your customer thinks that the results they can derive at point C are not worth the risks, they will probably decide to stay at point A. It is very important to ask questions like, "What is the downside of starting this project right now?" Or, "What do you see as some of the challenges in getting this done?"

You may not like everything you hear, but that's the whole point. Questions about risk help to reveal objections that your client might have or concerns that might hold them back from moving forward. We need to be willing to ask our customers the "tough" questions. If they do have concerns, then we can help them work things out. It also gives us a chance to explain what we can do to minimize any risks they might perceive in moving ahead with our proposed solution.

9. Solution Fit (B)

One criterion for gauging the probability of bringing an opportunity to closure is how well your B fits as a solution to help your customer achieve their desired business goals. Let's face it, your product or service doesn't fit every situation. Always ask your customer to share their vision of the ideal solution. After all, it's not your opinion of how well your solution fits but your customer's perception that matters.

If you ask the right questions, your customer might tell you exactly how to position your product or service to be a perfect fit. They could also describe a solution that is completely wrong or that perfectly resembles your competitor's offering. Using the results-based approach enables you to position your solution in the best possible light, but some situations are better suited for your solutions than others. If your product or service is simply a bad fit for your prospective customer, don't be too surprised if they decide not to buy.

10. Relationships

The quality of the business relationships you develop with your client is a major factor in winning sales opportunities. It appears as number 10 on the scorecard, but it can be just as important—or maybe more important—than any other factor. A relationship is typically not the *reason* a customer decides to buy, but it can have a huge influence on who they openly share information with and who they ultimately decide to buy from. The *quality* of your client relationships is important, but the *quantity* also matters. That's why we spend so much time in Chapter Four talking about building your relationship footprint.

Who you are dealing with and talking to within your customer's organization will determine the quality and quantity of the information you are able to gather. Therefore, your understanding of *why* they would buy and *how* they could buy is based on who you know within the account and how willing they are to work with you and share information. A highly qualified opportunity is one where you are given a chance to meet the people you need to meet and build the rapport necessary to win the business.

* * *

Qualifying sales opportunities involves asking a lot of questions. Of course, we can't sit our customer down and ask them a hundred questions in a row, so we need to learn to weave these questions into casual conversations. In fact, it may not be appropriate to ask questions about all these different elements of just one person.

You might want to ask questions about means and resources of the project owner, while reserving your questions about payback and return for the investment owner. It's best to ask several people the key questions about each element of why customers buy as you work through a sales cycle. That way, you can get multiple opinions and perspectives to add to your own understanding of why they would buy. Figure 5.3 will help you begin using these kinds of questions as soon as possible by providing several more sample questions for all 10 elements.

Qualifying How Customers Buy

Depending on the size and complexity of what you sell, your customer's buying process may involve several different influencers and approvers, dozens of decisions, and could take 6, 12, or even 18 months from start to finish. Selling inexpensive products or services in a transactional selling environment can be tough enough, but the more complex and expensive your solutions are, the more people and steps are involved.

The steps and stages of your customer's buying process will depend on several factors, including:

- Whether you are selling a product or a service.
- Whether you are selling to a new prospect or an existing customer.

Questions about Why Customers Buy

1. Current State (A)
How are things going? How happy are you with your results thus far?
How have things changed over the last 6 to 12 months?
How content are you with your current situation and outlook for the future?

2. Desired Future State (C)
Where do you plan to go from here? What are your plans moving forward?
If anything were possible, what changes would you most like to see?
In a perfect world, how would the current situation be different?

3. Motive
Why is achieving this desired result (goal or objective) so important?
Why is this project such a high priority right now?
Why would solving this problem be so valuable?

4. Urgency
When do you think you need to take action on this?
When would this project need to be completed?
When would you like to start seeing results?

5. Payback/Return
How much money could you save by _____?
How much time could you cut out of this process if _____?
How many more _____ could you _____ if _____?

6. Means/Resources
How could you obtain the funding for this project?
How would you justify an investment of this magnitude?
How would you staff a project like this if it were approved?

7. Consequence(s)
What would be the consequences of *not* taking action now?
What if you decided to put this project off until next year?
What would it cost you to put this off another month?

8. Risk(s)
What do you see as some of the risks involved in this project?
What are the obstacles to getting this done, as you see them?
Is there any downside to starting this project right away?

9. Solution Fit (B)
What do you envision as the ideal solution to solve this problem?
Have you given any thought to how this desired result could be achieved?
What is the best way to achieve this objective, in your opinion?

10. Relationships
If we had the right solution, would you consider doing business with us?
Is there any reason you couldn't or wouldn't want to do business with us?
Who else, besides us, would you consider partnering with on this project?

Available at: **SalesExcellence.com**

Figure 5.3 Questions About Why Customers Buy

- The corporate structure of the company you are selling to.
- The size of the financial investment or the impact of your solution.

Despite all these variables there are certain similarities in the steps that a typical customer must take in order to acquire the kinds of products and services you sell.

I have identified 10 elements that are part of most complex buying processes. These 10 make up criteria 11 through 20 of the opportunity scorecard. We should anticipate that our customer will have to work through each of these before they are ready to buy. They include:

11. Ownership/Oversight
12. Project prioritization
13. Organizational alignment
14. Staffing/Implementation plan
15. Financial approval
16. Solution approval
17. Legal/Contract approval
18. Vendor recommendation
19. Final approval
20. Purchase/Agreement

There are probably several individual steps your customer will have to take in order to obtain financial approval. There will also be several steps they need to take before the selection committee will be able to make their vendor recommendation. We need to start as early as possible in the sales cycle to understand *what* and *who* will be involved in working through each of these 10 elements. When your customer has worked through *all* of them, then and only then will they be ready and able to buy.

If these 10 elements don't exactly fit the environment you sell in, then use these as a starting place to create your own list of elements that do fit. As you learn the stages and steps involved in a typical buy-ing process for a customer in your market, you will become far more effective at qualifying each opportunity in your portfolio.

11. Ownership/Oversight

Perhaps the most essential element of a complex buying process is determining who will *own*—and provide *oversight* for—the success-ful use of the product or service and the achievement of the desired business results. This may be the responsibility of one person, per-haps the project owner, or some other person or committee who has the ultimate ownership.

To evaluate this element of an opportunity, we need to learn the answer to some key questions, such as: "Who will be responsible for overseeing the implementation and use of this solution?" Or, "Who will be responsible for earning a profit on the money and staffing resources that are invested?"

In a top-down buying decision, ownership or oversight is nor-mally established early on. On the other hand, in a bottom-up pro-cess, ownership and oversight may not be determined until much later—and maybe never. Rest assured that until someone within your client's organization stands up and accepts the responsibility for the purchase—and the project or initiative it is associated with—your sales opportunity is very unlikely to come to closure.

12. Project Prioritization

Hopefully, the purchase of your product or service is a critical part of an important project or initiative, but not every project gets funded, staffed, approved, and completed. Companies don't have unlimited resources. They have to prioritize how they use their money and their people to pursue their desired business results. Figure 5.4 shows an example of a list of prioritized goals and objectives your client might be trying to achieve.

Your customer will always have more good projects to invest in than there is time, money, or resources to invest. They can't afford to take action on every viable project or investment. Therefore, the question they must answer is not whether any particular investment is good or bad, but whether it is better or worse than every other possible use of available capital and resources. A line has to be drawn, which I call the line of available resources. Above the line are the projects and initiatives that *can* be staffed and funded and below it are others that *cannot*.

To be successful, we have to figure out how to get the project that our solutions are a part of *above* that line of available resources or focus on selling solutions tied to projects that are *already* above the line. Until I learned this, I spent years trying to sell solutions to problems that my customers never got around to solving. Understanding the other projects your client is currently considering—and how highly they prioritize the project you are part of—is an important aspect of qualifying any sales opportunity.

13. Organizational Alignment

Before a company will make a decision to buy, a number of people will have to agree that it is the right thing to do. Clem will need to believe that you are the best vendor with the best solution. His boss, Joe, will need to be ready to oversee the project. Joe's boss, the COO, must provide final approval for the investment. The CFO will have to be convinced that the project will achieve the return on investment promised.

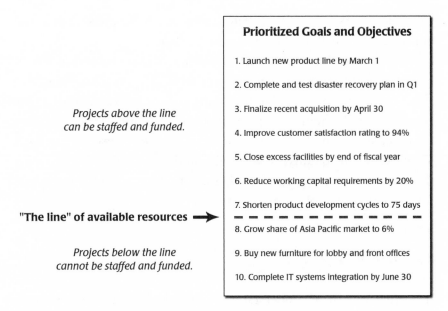

Projects above the line can be staffed and funded.

"The line" of available resources ➡

Projects below the line cannot be staffed and funded.

Prioritized Goals and Objectives

1. Launch new product line by March 1

2. Complete and test disaster recovery plan in Q1

3. Finalize recent acquisition by April 30

4. Improve customer satisfaction rating to 94%

5. Close excess facilities by end of fiscal year

6. Reduce working capital requirements by 20%

7. Shorten product development cycles to 75 days
— — — — — — — — — — — —
8. Grow share of Asia Pacific market to 6%

9. Buy new furniture for lobby and front offices

10. Complete IT systems integration by June 30

Figure 5.4 Your Customer's Prioritized Goals and Objectives

A certain level of cooperation across the organization is required for any buying process to result in a purchase. A vital part of our job is to do the selling required to get all the influencers and approvers aligned and ready to move forward. If we don't know who is playing which role in our customer's buying process or we don't know who's in support of moving forward, we don't know everything we need to know to properly qualify *how* they would buy.

14. Staffing/Implementation Plan

Many big-ticket purchases can't be approved until your customer has developed a plan of how the products or services being acquired will be used to get from point A to point C. Your customer may need to produce an implementation and staffing plan for the project your solutions are associated with before they obtain all the sign-offs and approvals they will need to make the purchase.

Some companies put this off until after they've gone through an elaborate evaluation and selection process. But the COO may not sign off until the project plan has been created and a feasibility study is completed. Without an implementation plan with a firm target date for completion, the CFO may not be willing to release the funding. We need to start qualifying very early in the sales cycle to determine if they've got the people and the bandwidth to take on the project or initiative that our solutions are associated with.

15. Financial Approval

It is crucial for us to understand the process our customer must go through to obtain the funding to buy what we are trying to sell. If they have a budget, that's good. But don't forget that budgeting is simply planning. The marketing department can plan to invest $100,000 in print advertising—they might even have the budget for it—but if the company doesn't have the money in their bank account or some way to finance it, the CFO or the controller can't provide financial approval.

To fully qualify an opportunity, we have to understand everything that has to happen before they can buy. We need to learn the answers to questions like these:

- Are they planning to add the purchase of our equipment to their expense budget?
- Do they have to submit a capital appropriation request (CAR)?
- What is the process for justifying the investment?
- Will they need to create an ROI analysis?

- Who will evaluate the ROI and what other investments or benchmarks will they compare it to?
- Who will actually release the funds for payment?

These are just a few of the questions that we have every right and every responsibility to ask as we evaluate and qualify an opportunity.

16. Solution Approval

Part of winning any sales opportunity involves obtaining solution approval. In essence, this means that Clem has looked at several different solutions from several different vendors and determined that your product and the professional services you provide will, in fact, get them from point A to point C. But that might not be all that is involved.

Solution approval also might require getting sign-off from the director of IT that your solution is compatible with their existing systems and meets certain standardization requirements. It could mean that the global sourcing department has added your company to their approved vendor list, and they have no problem buying from you instead of some other vendor. As you qualify each opportunity, consider how you are doing in the area of solution approval, not just with Clem, but with all the players involved.

17. Contract Approval

Getting your customer's legal department to review your contract or license agreement can be tedious, but failure to plan for this and anticipate potential objections can severely slow down or stall an opportunity. Nothing is more frustrating or risky than doing all the work it takes to win solution approval, negotiate the deal, and even get final approval, only to see the deal get hung up for 30 days while Legal fiddles around with the wording of a contract.

Start early in the sales cycle to ask about the process for getting your contract through your customer's legal department. Offer a sample copy of the terms and conditions to be looked at long before you get to the end of the buying process. Knowing what and who is involved in getting contract approval is an important element of sales qualification.

18. Vendor Recommendation

At some point in the buying process, the committee will probably recommend one vendor over all the others. At least we hope so. If what we sell is perceived as such a commodity that nobody cares where they buy it from, we are in trouble. If a purchase request is handed off to procurement with a list of vendors to buy from, prepare to lose the opportunity or make the sale at a tiny margin—if not a loss.

Be careful not to spend all your energy trying to win the recommendation with no regard for qualifying the other nine elements of how customers buy. Winning the coveted recommended vendor status is only *one* aspect of what it takes to bring a deal to closure, and thus one element against which we qualify each opportunity.

19. Final Approval

After the selection committee makes its recommendation, the project owner is onboard, and the organization is adequately aligned, the investment owner will still probably have to get final approval before she can move forward. It is very common, especially in large transactions, for the contract signer to need someone else's approval before they can sign. If you are selling to a division or a subsidiary of a larger company, they might need to go to Corporate to get final approval.

We need to understand how final approval is obtained and be convinced that it will happen before we can be confident that the deal will come to closure. Understanding the process and knowing the people involved is critical. An opportunity cannot be highly probable if we have never met those who will be involved in the final approval.

20. Purchase/Agreement

Assuming you do get the final approval, you may still have to get the deal through purchasing. This can be a very dangerous stage in a sales cycle. Procurement or global sourcing can sometimes take things in a totally different direction. We have to be smart and not assume that just because we are the vendor of choice when the purchase request gets to the procurement department that we are still the vendor of choice when the order is placed.

Don't wait until this point to start building a relationship with the purchasing manager. If you know the deal has to go to purchasing eventually, start early to meet the people in purchasing who may ultimately hold your destiny in their hands. Do your best to earn the right to meet all signatories—especially the ones who will sign the final agreement—long before you get to the later stages of the buying process.

* * *

To properly qualify a sales opportunity, you have to understand your customer's buying process by learning what has already happened and what still needs to happen. Figure 5.5 provides a list of questions that can help you remember what to ask when qualifying how your customer could buy. Remember that you need to know not just *what* is involved, but *who* is involved in every aspect of the process.

These questions will help you determine where your customer is in each of these 10 areas so you can thoroughly qualify the opportunity. In Chapter Six we go even deeper into understanding who and what is involved in your customer's overall buying process.

Scoring Prospective Sales Opportunities

The opportunity scorecard enables you to score your active sales opportunities on 20 different criteria that will help you determine the probability and closeability of each deal. Some selling systems try very hard to eliminate subjectivity and the personal judgment of the sales professional. This is impossible because as soon as you design a system that is rigid enough to eliminate all subjectivity, it is not flexible enough to account for all the shades of gray that are present in every buying process. I prefer to offer a set of specific guidelines for qualification and then *embrace* the judgment of the sales professional in scoring each opportunity.

Scoring Opportunities on Why

Before you begin scoring your customer on why they would buy, let's talk about how to evaluate and score each element. The scale for scoring is 0 to 5 (zero to five). Scoring a zero on desired future state, for example, means that you have not yet talked to your customer

Questions about How Customers Buy

11. Ownership/Oversight
Who has the ultimate responsibility for the success of this project (purchase)?
Who will provide executive-level oversight for the project?
Who will be responsible for the return on investment for this purchase?

12. Project Prioritization
How do you determine which projects are ultimately staffed and funded?
How does this project rank compared to others under consideration?
Which other projects (purchases) would take precedence over this one?

13. Organizational Alignment
How well aligned is senior management in support of this project (purchase)?
Which other departments, units, or senior managers need to be on board?
How do you plan to build a consensus for moving forward?

14. Staffing/Implementation Plan
What is involved in staffing (implementing) a project such as this one?
Who would be responsible for planning and overseeing the implementation?
Who would have to approve the staffing and implementation plan?

15. Financial Approval
How will you fund this project (purchase)? How will you justify the investment?
What is the process of getting financial approval for this project (purchase)?
Do you already have a budget? What must happen before funds can be released?

16. Solution Approval
What is your process for determining which solution is the best fit for you?
Who would be involved in the evaluation, selection, and approval processes?
Which other people or departments will need to approve your solution of choice?

17. Legal/Contract Approval
What is involved in getting a contract approved by your legal department?
Who will have to approve the terms and conditions of our contract (agreement)?
Can we put a copy of our terms and conditions in front of your legal department?

18. Vendor Recommendation
What criteria will you use to select the right partner for this project?
What are the most important characteristics of your ideal vendor (supplier)?
Once you select your vendor of choice, who else will have a say in the matter?

19. Final Approval
What is the process of getting final approval for a project (investment) like this?
Who provides final approval for a project (investment) like this?
Will you need to go to your parent corporation (board of directors) for approval?

20. Purchase/Agreement
What is involved in getting something like this through purchasing?
How can we apply to be considered for your approved vendor list?
If we get that far, who would release the purchase order (execute the agreement)?

Available at: **SalesExcellence.com**

Figure 5.5 Questions About How Customers Buy

about the business results they want to accomplish. A zero on consequences means that you have no idea whether your customer will experience any negative effects by delaying or forgoing the purchase of your products or services. It can also mean that you have discussed it but there are no real consequences if they delay.

Work through the scorecard, evaluating your opportunity on each element. If you've never even brought up the subject with your client, it's a zero. If you've asked Clem about it and he has no clue, it's *still* a zero. To score anything greater than zero requires a conversation with your customer.

To get an idea of what it takes to score a perfect 5 on any particular criterion, please refer to the opportunity scorecard guidelines 1–10 in Figure 5.6. Take the time to get familiar with what it takes to score a 5 on each criterion. The guidelines are quite strict, and scoring a 5 on any of these 10 elements will require significant work on your part.

Using the guidelines as a frame of reference and using your own best judgment, determine how your prospect scores in each of these 10 areas. Remember, this is not an evaluation of the salesperson managing the account. A low score on any particular criterion doesn't necessarily reflect badly on you as a salesperson. We are trying to evaluate the true quality of the opportunity at this time and determine what we need to do next to make it better.

Scoring Opportunities on How

Evaluating sales opportunities on *how* your customer would buy requires a great deal more objectivity than evaluating a deal on why. When we qualify on why, we are gauging how our customer thinks or feels. We ask ourselves questions like, "Do they have a clear vision

Opportunity Scorecard Guidelines 1-10

Scoring a perfect "5" means...

1. Current State (A)

You have completed the company research template and have a good understanding of where each of the approvers and major influencers believes they are right now (point A). All approvers and influencers are *not* content to stay where they are now.

2. Desired Future State (C)

All the approvers and major influencers have a clear vision of their ideal point C. You understand the outcomes or results each of them wants to achieve at point C and you are confident you can help them achieve those results.

3. Motive

Each of the approvers and major influencers is driven to take action to achieve their desired outcomes and results. You understand *why* they want to achieve these results and how each result ties back to their corporate goals and objectives.

4. Urgency

All the approvers and major influencers agree on a specific date *when* they absolutely must reach point C to satisfy a promise they have made to their customers, employees, shareholders, the government, or some other stakeholder of the company.

5. Payback/Return

You have worked with your customer to determine the payback or return on investment (*how much* or *how many*) they expect once they arrive at point C. All approvers and major influencers agree that the return is well worth the investment of time and money.

6. Means/Resources

You and all your customer's approvers and major influencers know exactly *how* they plan to pay for your solution and provide whatever additional resources (such as staffing and infrastructure) they will need to get to point C on time and on budget.

7. Consequence(s)

You and all your customer's approvers and major influencers know exactly what bad thing(s) will happen—or what it will cost them—if they don't get to point C on time and on budget. Everyone agrees that they absolutely must avoid those consequences.

8. Risk(s)

You and all your customer's approvers and major influencers understand the risks involved in making the investment and taking action to pursue their C at this time. Everyone agrees that the value of reaching point C is well worth the associated risks.

9. Solution Fit (B)

You have worked with each of the approvers and major influencers to understand and develop their vision of the ideal solution. You believe—and are able to prove—that you can deliver it and then help them use it to get to point C on time and on budget.

10. Relationships

You have met or spoken with all the approvers and major influencers involved in this particular buying process. You have identified each on your buying roles chart. Each has indicated a preference for doing business with you as opposed to any other vendor.

Available at: **SalesExcellence.com**

Figure 5.6 Opportunity Scorecard Guidelines 1–10

of their desired future state (C)?" Or, "Do they have a strong sense of urgency?" However, when we qualify on *how*, we are evaluating how well we understand each element of our customer's buying process as well as what steps they have taken so far.

As you did with the first 10, evaluate each element on the *how* side of the scorecard on a scale of 0 to 5. A zero means that you either have no idea what is involved in obtaining financial approval, for example, or you have talked to your client about the process, but they have taken no steps of any kind to obtain funding. Use the opportunity scorecard guidelines 11–20 in Figure 5.7 as your yardstick to determine what your customer has accomplished thus far in their buying process. Then, score the opportunity on each element of how they would buy.

I encourage you to go through your entire opportunity portfolio scoring each deal using these guidelines. Once you determine the real quality of each opportunity, the decision of where to invest your time for maximum revenue results becomes much easier to make.

The Opportunity Scorecard in Action

Once you have scored a sales opportunity on all 20 elements of the opportunity scorecard, you can add them up to arrive at a total probability out of 100. This number represents the overall quality of the opportunity and the probability or likelihood that the opportunity will come to closure. Now your scorecard will probably look something like the example shown in Figure 5.8 on page 123.

The quality or probability of an opportunity is actually only a perception that is based on our limited understanding of how and why our customer would buy. Our perception can change in an instant when we meet the CEO who tells us, "Although Clem is focused on

Opportunity Scorecard Guidelines 11-20

Scoring a perfect "5" means...

11. Ownership/Oversight

You have identified who will be the *project owner* and the *investment owner* associated with the purchase of your solution. You have met with each of them and have obtained buy-in, commitment, and strong support from both.

12. Project Prioritization

The project, which the purchase of your solution is part of, is a high priority for all the approvers and major influencers involved in the buying decision. It is—and will remain—*above the line* of available resources and represents a better investment than the other projects competing for available capital and resources.

13. Organizational Alignment

All the approvers and major influencers involved in your customer's buying decision are aligned in their support for moving forward with the project and the purchase at this time.

14. Staffing/Implementation Plan

The *project owner* and the other approvers and major influencers have agreed on how the associated project will be staffed and have defined and agreed on an implementation plan. The required staffing for the project has been allocated and approved.

15. Financial Approval

You have identified who will be the *financial approver*. The investment in your solution and the associated project has been evaluated, justified, and approved. They have released or committed all required funding or have secured and obtained proper financing.

16. Solution Approval

You have identified who will be the *solution approver*. They have concluded that your solution meets all the necessary specifications and requirements and have approved your product or service as the solution of choice.

17. Legal/Contract Approval

You have identified who will be the *legal/contract approver*. They have reviewed and approved all the terms and conditions of your contract or agreement. It is ready to be signed or executed.

18. Vendor Recommendation

You have identified who will be the *recommender(s)* or the members of the vendor selection committee. They have selected your company as the vendor of choice to provide the required product or services solution and have submitted their recommendation for approval.

19. Final Approval

You have identified who will be the *final approver(s)*. They have authorized the execution of the final contract or agreement and forwarded the purchase request or contract to the purchasing department or contract signer for completion.

20. Purchase/Agreement

You have identified who will be the *contract signer* and they have executed the final contract. Or . . . The *buyer* (i.e., purchasing, procurement, or strategic sourcing) has released the purchase order and processed the order for payment.

Available at: **SalesExcellence.com**

Figure 5.7 Opportunity Scorecard Guidelines 11–20

buying new equipment for the laboratory, my primary objective is to cut costs by outsourcing all laboratory functions to a third party." Our customer's reality can also change quickly when the CFO decides to put a freeze on all purchases until further notice.

The probability of an opportunity is a very fluid measure. Part of our job is to evaluate the quality of the opportunity frequently so we always know where things stand. But another part of our job is to do all that we can to try to improve the quality of the opportunity as we go along.

Let's imagine that you used the opportunity scorecard to qualify a deal, and scored it at 56. The question is whether the deal is destined to forever be a 56, or whether we can turn it into a 78 by meeting more people, asking more questions, and helping our customer take the steps they need to take in their buying process. Using the opportunity scorecard will guide you in your efforts to make the most of every sales opportunity.

A participant in one of my workshops in London asked, "If you know for sure that you are going to get the order, do you still need to spend all this time doing all of this qualification stuff?" That's an interesting question.

I suppose if you had some way of knowing "for sure" that you were going to win a given sales opportunity, then you would have no reason to qualify. However, I wonder how a salesperson would conclude that they were "for sure" going to get the order in the first place.

I suspect that it would have to be a client that had a strong relationship with you and your company. The client would have to know exactly why they were buying, how they would use your product or service in their business, and have a reason to buy in a certain time frame. They would obviously have to possess the resources to buy and believe that the investment in your solution would provide a favorable return.

Opportunity Scorecard

Date: _Apr 19_

Account: _Delcom Technologies_   Opportunity: _Inventory Mgmt. System_

Why would they buy?	Score each 0 to 5	How could they buy?	Score each 0 to 5
1. Current State (A)	4	11. Ownership/Oversight	3
2. Desired Future State (C)	3	12. Project Prioritization	1
3. Motive	4	13. Organizational Alignment	3
4. Urgency	2	14. Staffing/Implementation Plan	2
5. Payback/Return	2	15. Financial Approval	3
6. Means/Resources	3	16. Solution Approval	4
7. Consequence(s)	2	17. Legal/Contract Approval	0
8. Risk(s)	1	18. Vendor Recommendation	3
9. Solution Fit (B)	3	19. Final Approval	2
10. Relationships	3	20. Purchase/Agreement	1

Why Subtotal: _27_

How Subtotal: _22_

Total Probability out of 100: _49_

Available at: **SalesExcellence.com**

Using the opportunity scorecard guidelines and your own best judgment, determine how your opportunity scores on each of the 20 criteria.

The scorecard helps you discover potential weaknesses in sales opportunities while you still have time to do something about them.

The total score from the scorecard can be used to calculate weighted probability for sales forecasting.

Figure 5.8 The Opportunity Scorecard in Action

If you knew "for sure" that you were going to get the order, it would be because you have met with the people within your client's company who will oversee the use of whatever it is that you sell. You would have knowledge of their buying process and the various influencers and approvers involved. You would also know, probably from prior experience, what it takes—and how long it takes—to get an order initiated, approved, and processed through their organization.

In short, you would know "for sure" that you would get the order because you had thoroughly qualified the opportunity! Experienced salespeople are constantly qualifying and requalifying sales opportunities, whether they consciously realize it or not. Of course many things could change that would interrupt the buying process. So I don't see how any of us could ever know "for sure" that we would receive any given order. But asking the right questions to better understand why your customer would buy and how they could buy if they wanted to helps you focus your efforts where you are most likely to reap a substantial return.

* * *

Using the opportunity scorecard—along with its associated questions and guidelines—offers a systematic approach for qualifying sales opportunities. It helps less experienced salespeople remember all the criteria for qualifying an opportunity as well as the questions they need to ask as they help their clients work through the buying process. It also helps more experienced salespeople become more efficient and consistent so they can maximize their sales capacity and manage more opportunities at once. More effective qualification leads to higher success rates and more accurate forecasting, and ensures that you are doing all you can to maximize your sales results.

CHAPTER SIX

Structuring and Accelerating Sales Opportunities

All sales opportunities are *not* created equal. Some are good, some are great, and some are downright terrible. We have to be very careful about which deals we choose to invest our time in if we want to maximize our sales results. We have to understand enough about a particular customer's buying process—and the people who are involved in that process—to structure the opportunity so that we can reliably determine *if* it will close and *when* it will close.

Structuring a sales opportunity actually starts from the very first conversation with our prospect. It is part of the ongoing process of sales qualification and should be done anytime you detect a change in your customer's buying process. We continually evaluate and reevaluate where our customer is within their process and what additional steps they need to take before they can buy.

Chapter Three deals with filling your sales portfolio so you have plenty of opportunities to choose from. Chapter Five focuses on qualifying sales opportunities so you know which deals to invest your time in and what to do to improve the quality of each opportunity. This chapter addresses how to structure and manage your opportunities in order to increase sales velocity and improve sales predictability.

We start by discussing how to establish a time frame for a sales opportunity. We explore the concept of reverse-engineering and how you can use this practice to better understand all the things that would have to happen before your customer could buy. We talk about how to turn your knowledge of your customer's buying process into a joint plan for moving forward together. Then we look at several tools and techniques you can use to accelerate your customer's buying process and accomplish as much as possible during every phone call or meeting.

Framing the Sales Opportunity

Structuring a sales opportunity begins with what I call *framing* the opportunity. Framing binds the opportunity in time by establishing a time frame for helping your customer achieve their desired business results and arrive at point C. Let's begin this discussion by taking another look at the customer results model in Figure 6.1.

To help our customer get from point A (their current state) to point C (their desired future state), there are two distinct processes we have to help them work through. The first is their overall buying process—all the little decisions and steps they must take as they work through evaluation, selection, approval, and purchasing. The second is their utilization process—everything they have to do to install, integrate, implement, and use our product or service to obtain their desired business results.

By nature, business customers—and especially executives—are very results-oriented. Their perception of time is not based on when they are planning to purchase some product or service. They think in terms of when they can start reaping the business benefits of using that product or service to achieve their desired business results.

When we ask questions like, "When do you plan to make the purchase?" Or, "When do you plan to make your decision?" it only

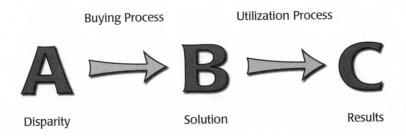

Figure 6.1 The Processes That Lead to Point C

serves to illustrate how out of touch we are with how customers think. Sure, we want to know when they plan to buy our B. But what our customer is focused on is when they can reliably expect to arrive at point C. Using the results-based approach, we need to figure out what outcomes or results our customer is focused on achieving—and when they need to achieve them—so we can focus our attention there too.

Once we know when our customer wants to, needs to, or absolutely has to get to point C, then we can put together a reliable plan to help them get there. Part of that plan will involve the purchase of our products or services. But what defines the time frame of the purchase is their time frame for achieving their desired business results.

Questions for Framing the Opportunity

To establish the time frame of a sales opportunity, we ask our customer specific questions that relate to the six action drivers which we discuss in Chapter Two. Three of the six are especially important in framing the opportunity: urgency, motive, and consequence.

1. Urgency: "When Do You Have to Achieve Your Desired Result?" This question could also be phrased, "When do you need to have this project completed?" or, "When do you need to start seeing results?" However you choose to ask it, find out when your customer has to get to point C. I emphasize "has to" because if they only want to, or need to, that might not be enough to prioritize this purchase or project above all the others under consideration.

What we hope to hear is a firm date by which our customer needs to begin to see the business results they are hoping for. If the person you are dealing with doesn't have a firm date in mind, you have work to do. You will have to help them perceive an urgency to get to C by a certain point in time or find someone else within the organization who does see the urgency.

Let's assume for a moment that the person you are qualifying does have a time frame for getting to point C and he or she tells you, "We need to get this purchase completed and the system up and running by September 30." You still have a few important questions to ask.

2. Motive: "Why Do You Have to Achieve Your Desired Result by Then?" Assuming that your customer has a date in mind for arriving at C, now you need to find out why they picked that specific date. If they identified September 30, for example, ask them, "Why do you say September 30?" and maybe follow that question with, "Why would you want to wait until September 30? Would July 31 or August 31 be better?" This is an attempt to explore the possibility of accelerating the buying process.

What we are looking for is a strong reason why they need to get to C by September 30. Ideally, we'll hear about a promise they have made to their biggest customer or a new government regulation that goes into effect by a certain time. If the customer doesn't have a strong motive that is tied to a specific date, the opportunity could easily slip from one month to the next indefinitely.

3. Consequence: "What If You Don't Achieve Your Desired Result by Then?" With this question we are probing for a consequence related to inaction. Without some consequence, most customers won't buy anything. You can't blame them. You'd do the same thing in their place. But maybe by engaging them in conversation we can help them explore a consequence they hadn't thought about before.

Many customers put off the purchase to the point that there isn't sufficient time to get things delivered, installed, and implemented before the date that they have to arrive at C. That's one of the reasons why framing the opportunity is so important. Your customer isn't done when they release a purchase order for your solution. By focusing on their time frame for getting to C, you demonstrate your interest in partnering with them to achieve their desired results.

Asking questions that begin with "When ... ?" "Why ... ?" and, "What if you don't ... ?" helps you understand the urgency, motive, and consequence at play in your customer's buying decision. But it is helpful to ask additional questions about the other action drivers as well.

Revisit their expectations for payback and return by asking, "If you could get this done by then, what would you expect in terms of payback or return on investment?" You can double-check the availability of means and resources with a question like, "How will you secure the resources in terms of staffing and funding to get this done by then?" Also don't forget to revisit risk by asking, "What do you see as the challenges to getting this done by then?"

All these questions will help you get a better feel for how important and realistic the September 30 date actually is. Figure 6.2 lists some of the questions you can ask as you attempt to frame an opportunity with your customer.

Remember to qualify and frame your opportunity with as many different people as possible within your customer's organization. Get

Questions for Framing the Opportunity

Urgency
When do you have to achieve your desired result?

Motive
Why do you have to achieve your desired result by then?

Consequence(s)
What if you don't achieve your desired result by then?

Payback/Return
If you could achieve your desired result by then, what would you expect in terms of payback or return on investment?

Means/Resources
How will you secure the resources in terms of staffing and funding to achieve your desired result by then?

Risk(s)
What do you see as the challenges of—or obstacles to—achieving your desired result by then?

Available at: **SalesExcellence.com**

Figure 6.2 Questions for Framing the Opportunity

a complete understanding of urgency, motive, and consequence from several people—especially the project owner, the investment owner, and whoever will provide final approval.

It is important to point out that if an opportunity cannot be framed, it doesn't mean we should just walk away from it. Maybe with a little work we could help to uncover or create an urgency. If we can meet more people within the company, perhaps we can find someone who better recognizes the urgency to reach point C or who can envision a different point C that *is* more urgent.

Framing the opportunity is essential to structuring the deal to close. It is probably safe to say that if we don't find an urgency, motive and consequence that are tied to a specific date for getting to point C, forecasting the opportunity to close in a certain time frame is little more than wishful thinking.

Reverse-Engineering the Buying Process

Once we've framed the sales opportunity, we can work with our customer to construct a timeline that gets them from where they are today to where they want to be by the time they have to be there. I call this reverse-engineering the buying process. Since we start at point C and work backward, we will actually create the timeline in reverse.

We start by framing the opportunity with a target date to arrive at point C. Then, we explore what will be involved in installing, implementing, and using our solution to get to C. This portion of the overall journey to C is a critical part of your customer's success. They can buy products and services all day long, but until they use them to pursue some specific business results, those products and services are investments that never deliver a return.

I have found that until your customer knows exactly what is involved in getting from B to C, they will not be willing to move from A to B. Reverse-engineering the utilization process (from B to C) helps your customer identify when they will need to sign your contract or place the order. Then you can work with them to complete the plan by defining the timeline of the buying process (from A to B).

The Reverse-Engineering Worksheet

The reverse-engineering worksheet, shown in Figure 6.3, is an excellent tool to help facilitate the discussion about your plan to help your customer get to point C. Begin at the bottom of the worksheet by framing the opportunity and identifying your customer's target date to arrive at point C. Then you can explore the various steps, events, milestones, or decisions that your customer will encounter as they move from where they are now (A) all the way to point C.

Be careful not to overwhelm your customer by trying to complete this entire worksheet on your very first meeting or phone call.

Understanding a complex buying process takes time. You will probably have to talk to several different people to get the complete picture of everything that will have to happen before your customer can buy.

As you work with your client to build the plan, identify the people within your customer's organization who should be involved in each of these steps. This is one of the techniques you will use to grow your relationship footprint and gain access to all the key players involved in the buying process.

The worksheet includes a list of the 10 elements involved in a complex buying decision (from A to B). There is also a list of some of the events that might need to take place during their utilization process between B and C. These will help prompt you during your discussion with your customer.

Hypothetical Questions about the Buying Process

Hypothetical questions, which are introduced in Chapter Five as a way to explore your customer's point C, are also extremely useful as you reverse-engineer your customer's buying process. Keep your questions very conversational and weave them into your discussion so that it doesn't feel like an interrogation. Here are a few examples:

- Let's say we go through this discovery process together, and you decide that our solution is just the right fit for you. What happens then?
- Let's assume for a minute that your boss was onboard with the project. What other approvals would be needed?
- If we get that far, who would actually sign the contract?

Figure 6.4 on page 135 shows many more examples of how you can use hypothetical questions to help you learn what is involved in your

Reverse-Engineering Worksheet

	Step, event, milestone or decision to be made.	Who will be involved?	When does this need to be done?
A			
Ownership/ Oversight	Needs Analysis	Project Team Jamal Sancar	March or April
Project Prioritization	Complete Product Demo	Selection Committee Karen Mercier	During April
Organizational Alignment	Submit Proposal	Project Lead and Boss David Park COO	Before May 1
Staffing/ Implementation	Provide References	Project Lead Jamal Sancar	With Proposal
Financial Approval	Select Vendor	Selection Committee Karen Mercier	Early May
Solution Approval	Project Approval	COO David Park and CIO Ed Crantz	Early May
Legal Approval	Financial Approval	CFO Alice Jurez	Mid-May
Vendor Recommen- dation	Executive Committee Approval	CEO Rod Harris	End of May
Final Approval	Review Agreement	CFO Alice Jurez	End of May
Purchase/ Agreement			
B	Finalize Agreement	COO David Park	By June 1
Delivery	Implementation Planning Meeting	Park, Sancar, Crantz, and Mercier	Early June
Installation	Finalize System Requirements	Jamal Sancar and Karen Mercier	Mid-June
Customization	System Customization	Karen Mercier and Steve Rossi	Late-June
Implemen- tation	Integrate with Existing Systems	Karen Mercier and Steve Rossi	By Mid-July
Integration	System Pilot Testing	Jamal Sancar and Karen Mercier	By End of July
Testing	Train System Users	User Community	Mid-August
Training	Go Live	User Community	End of August
C	Cut Product Test Cycles by 50%	Corporate Objective	September 30

Available at: **SalesExcellence.com**

Figure 6.3 The Reverse-Engineering Worksheet

customer's buying process. Try mixing and matching the various ways of setting up the hypothetical and exploring the process of moving forward. You might even want to have a mock discussion with your boss or a coworker, but make yourself comfortable with as many of these as possible so you will be more likely to weave them into conversations with your customers.

Start asking questions about your customer's buying process from the very first meeting or phone call. Many salespeople leave the tough questions, such as, "Who will sign the contract?" or, "How will the purchase be financed?" until the very end of the sales cycle. But something changes psychologically when your customer nears the end of their buying process. They get tense. Their aversion to risk sets in, and they start preparing to fend off any attempts you may make to close the deal. It's actually much easier to ask the tough questions early in the sales cycle, especially if you pose them in a hypothetical fashion.

The Customer Results Plan

When you have a good understanding of your customer's buying process and their utilization process, you can take what you've learned from your reverse-engineering worksheet and turn it into what I call a customer results plan. This is a project plan that outlines all the events and milestones you will pass through as you help your customer get from A to C. The plan should list all the people who will be involved in each step—both from your company and from your client's organization. The plan also shows the target date for each step as shown in Figure 6.5.

Your customer results plan will become a living document that changes and grows as you help your customer work through their buying process. You'll probably have to add events or readjust dates

Hypothetical Questions about the Buying Process

Set Up the Hypothetical	Explore the Process of Moving Forward
If you were in a position to move forward now . . .	Who would provide oversight for the project?
If you had already decided who would own the project . . .	What would be the next step?
What if you did get the support of upper management . . .	How would this project be staffed?
Imagine that you decided to prioritize this project and that your staffing and implementation plans were in place . . .	What's involved in getting something like this approved?
Assuming your boss and her boss were totally on board . . .	What do you think would happen then?
Suppose, after exploring your options, you concluded that we were the best company to partner with on this project . . .	What is the process of justifying an investment of this magnitude?
If the committee recommended us as the vendor of choice . . .	Who else would have a say in the matter?
Let's imagine that you got approval on the funding . . .	What other approvals would be needed?
Let's suppose you didn't get any objections from Legal . . .	What does the rest of the process entail?
Let's assume that our proof of concept was successful . . .	Who would provide the final approval?
Let's say that Corporate gave you the final approval . . .	What steps in the process would still remain?
If the purchase request makes it to procurement . . .	Who would actually issue the purchase order?

Available at: **Sales Excellence.com**

Figure 6.4 Hypothetical Questions about the Buying Process

as the sales cycle moves along. This type of plan is an extremely effective tool for managing a complex sales opportunity.

The Power of the Customer Results Plan

There are many ways in which the customer results plan improves opportunity management:

1. It Helps Keep You on Track. Developing a plan will make you more effective as you work through the steps and stages of a sales opportunity. It will also help you manage more opportunities simultaneously.

2. It Forces You to Look Ahead. Having a plan makes you think about the next step as well as other steps to follow. You can work through a process much faster if you don't have to make it up as you go along.

3. It Helps You to Stay Aligned with Your Buyer. When you work with your client to put together an engagement plan, you both know exactly where you are at all times. This reduces the chances of arriving at the end of your sales process only to find that your customer is still back at the beginning of their buying process.

4. It's a Tremendous Qualification Tool. When you share your plan with your client, you'll be able to tell immediately whether they are serious about doing business with you. Some won't even have the conversation. Others will yawn and change the subject. But the ones who like your plan will often take part ownership and help you figure out exactly what needs to happen, when it needs to happen, and who needs to be involved in each step in order to reach point C on time and on budget.

5. It Helps to Justify Access to the Right Executives. Planning out the steps of your customer's buying process and determining who the people are that need to be involved helps to justify why you should be given the chance to engage certain executives and other members of your customer's staff. The people within your customer's organization

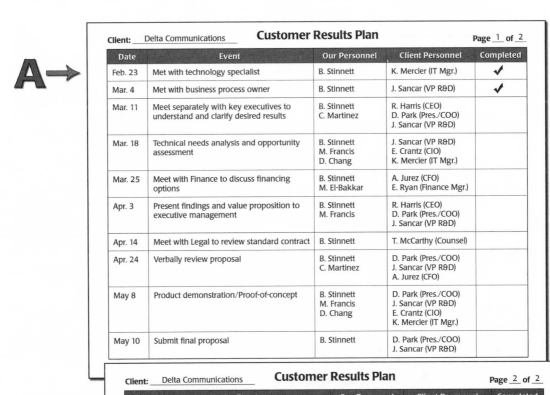

Customer Results Plan

Client: Delta Communications   Page 1 of 2

Date	Event	Our Personnel	Client Personnel	Completed
Feb. 23	Met with technology specialist	B. Stinnett	K. Mercier (IT Mgr.)	✔
Mar. 4	Met with business process owner	B. Stinnett	J. Sancar (VP R&D)	✔
Mar. 11	Meet separately with key executives to understand and clarify desired results	B. Stinnett C. Martinez	R. Harris (CEO) D. Park (Pres./COO) J. Sancar (VP R&D)	
Mar. 18	Technical needs analysis and opportunity assessment	B. Stinnett M. Francis D. Chang	J. Sancar (VP R&D) E. Crantz (CIO) K. Mercier (IT Mgr.)	
Mar. 25	Meet with Finance to discuss financing options	B. Stinnett M. El-Bakkar	A. Jurez (CFO) E. Ryan (Finance Mgr.)	
Apr. 3	Present findings and value proposition to executive management	B. Stinnett M. Francis	R. Harris (CEO) D. Park (Pres./COO) J. Sancar (VP R&D)	
Apr. 14	Meet with Legal to review standard contract	B. Stinnett	T. McCarthy (Counsel)	
Apr. 24	Verbally review proposal	B. Stinnett C. Martinez	D. Park (Pres./COO) J. Sancar (VP R&D) A. Jurez (CFO)	
May 8	Product demonstration/Proof-of-concept	B. Stinnett M. Francis D. Chang	D. Park (Pres./COO) J. Sancar (VP R&D) E. Crantz (CIO) K. Mercier (IT Mgr.)	
May 10	Submit final proposal	B. Stinnett	D. Park (Pres./COO) J. Sancar (VP R&D)	

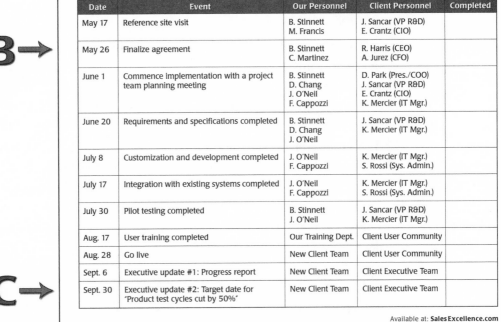

Customer Results Plan

Client: Delta Communications   Page 2 of 2

Date	Event	Our Personnel	Client Personnel	Completed
May 17	Reference site visit	B. Stinnett M. Francis	J. Sancar (VP R&D) E. Crantz (CIO)	
May 26	Finalize agreement	B. Stinnett C. Martinez	R. Harris (CEO) A. Jurez (CFO)	
June 1	Commence implementation with a project team planning meeting	B. Stinnett D. Chang J. O'Neil F. Cappozzi	D. Park (Pres./COO) J. Sancar (VP R&D) E. Crantz (CIO) K. Mercier (IT Mgr.)	
June 20	Requirements and specifications completed	B. Stinnett D. Chang J. O'Neil	J. Sancar (VP R&D) K. Mercier (IT Mgr.)	
July 8	Customization and development completed	J. O'Neil F. Cappozzi	K. Mercier (IT Mgr.) S. Rossi (Sys. Admin.)	
July 17	Integration with existing systems completed	J. O'Neil F. Cappozzi	K. Mercier (IT Mgr.) S. Rossi (Sys. Admin.)	
July 30	Pilot testing completed	B. Stinnett J. O'Neil	J. Sancar (VP R&D) K. Mercier (IT Mgr.)	
Aug. 17	User training completed	Our Training Dept.	Client User Community	
Aug. 28	Go live	New Client Team	Client User Community	
Sept. 6	Executive update #1: Progress report	New Client Team	Client Executive Team	
Sept. 30	Executive update #2: Target date for "Product test cycles cut by 50%"	New Client Team	Client Executive Team	

Available at: **SalesExcellence.com**

Figure 6.5 The Customer Results Plan

who buy in to your joint plan will usually help you meet all the people you need to meet.

6. Finalizing the Agreement Is Just One Step along the Way. When you develop a plan of how you will work with your client to get from point A *all the way* to point C, finalizing the agreement becomes just another step along the way. It eliminates a lot of the pressure and stress and puts the purchase in the context of how it will help your customer achieve their desired business results.

Troubleshooting the Customer Results Plan

If your prospective customer doesn't get excited about the plan you've developed, it usually has something to do with one or more of the following six issues:

1. The Plan Isn't Right. Sometimes the plan we propose just doesn't fit our customer's buying process, or the timing of the plan isn't right. You might need to work with your customer to tweak it or change it to better fit their internal processes and their time frame.

2. Someone Has Confused B with C. When you develop your customer results plan, always make sure you start at point C and work backward to A. If you start at A and work forward, it's too tempting for both you and your customer to start focusing on the features and functions of B rather than on the business value your customer will derive from arriving at point C.

3. Point C Isn't Right. Building your plan to help Clem arrive at his ideal point C might not be that compelling for his boss or the CFO of his company. Make sure your plan is designed to appeal to as many of the influencers and approvers involved in your customer's buying process as possible.

4. *They Would Rather Work the Plan with Someone Else.* There will be times when you do everything exactly right, but your customer still won't embrace your plan. Maybe another supplier provided a plan or a solution that is more closely aligned with their vision of the ideal C.

5. *You Are Proposing Your Plan to the Wrong Person.* To get buy-in and commitment to your plan, you will have to propose it to someone who has the authority to make a commitment to work with you.

6. *The Next Step You Are Proposing Isn't the "Next" Step.* If your client likes your plan, but isn't ready to more forward, there might be some additional steps that need to take place before they can commit to work the plan with you. If you can find out what that is, add that new step to your plan and propose moving forward once again.

Ongoing Opportunity Management

To increase sales velocity and improve sales predictability, you have to make the most of every client meeting and phone call. This requires forethought and planning, but the impact you will see in your sales results is well worth the effort.

Investing even a few minutes to review what has happened so far in each opportunity and then giving some thought to what needs to happen going forward can pay huge dividends. Our goal should be to move the sales opportunity forward with every meeting and phone call. This can be accomplished with some simple opportunity review and precall planning.

Opportunity Review

The first step in ongoing opportunity management is to determine where you stand by conducting an opportunity review. Whether you've been helping your customer work through their buying process for some time or you have just had your first meeting, take a moment to review everything that has happened and everything you've learned about this opportunity up to this point.

It is important to do an opportunity review before you do a precall plan. This serves the same purpose as finding the little dot on a wall map that shows, "You are here." You can't very well plan where you need to go next if you don't know where you are now. Take a minute to read through the opportunity review sheet in Figure 6.6.

The top section of this sheet helps you evaluate who you've met, where they are (A), where they want to go (C), and the action drivers that determine their desire to get there. The 10 questions align with the 10 elements of why customers buy that appear on the opportunity scorecard, which is presented in Chapter Five.

The lower section contains those four all-important questions from Chapter Two that help you pinpoint where your customer is within their buying process. This helps you determine what you need to do to help your customer take the next reasonable step. Perhaps the most important question is the last one on the sheet, "Who else do we need to meet with or speak to?" This is a reminder that you should constantly seek to broaden your relationship footprint.

Precall Planning

The precall planning sheet, shown in Figure 6.7 on page 143, is designed to help you plan exactly what you want to accomplish in your next meeting or phone call. Start by revisiting the opportunity review

Opportunity Review Sheet

Date: _____

Account: _____   Opportunity: _____

Who have we met with or spoken to?

What do we know about . . .

Their **Current State (A)** (i.e., needs, problems, pains, or disparities)?

Their **Desired Future State (C)** (i.e., goals, plans, or objectives)?

Their **Motive(s)** for achieving them?

Their **Urgency** to achieve them?

The **Payback** or **Return** they want or expect?

The **Means** or **Resources** they can make available?

The **Consequence(s)** of not achieving them?

The **Risk(s)** they see in pursuing them?

Their vision of the ideal **Solution (B)**?

Their **Relationships** to us or to other vendors being considered?

What do we know about . . .

1. This *particular* buying process (evaluation, selection, approval, purchasing)?
   Refer to 11-20 on the opportunity scorecard and incorporate all into the customer results plan.

2. Where the customer currently is within their buying process?

3. The next *reasonable* step the customer needs to take?

4. What we can do to help the customer take that step?

Who else do we need to meet with or speak to?

Available at: **Sales Excellence.com**

Figure 6.6 Opportunity Review Sheet

sheet to determine where you are. Then give some thought to what you plan to ask, say, or do in your next meeting to get a better understanding of how and why your customer would buy and move the opportunity forward.

The lower section of the precall planning sheet gets to the heart of the matter by asking, "What is the purpose of this meeting or phone call?" and "What specific step do we want our customer to take during or after the meeting?" among other things. You are far more likely to move the opportunity in a positive direction if you go into your meeting or make your phone call with a game plan and a desired outcome in mind.

These two sheets are designed to help you think about what you want to accomplish in your next meeting or phone call and gather the information you will need to complete an opportunity scorecard for each account. Using the scorecard will help reveal which aspects of *why* and *how* your customer would buy that you need to know more about.

If you are thinking that you don't have time to fill out these forms because you are already too busy, let me emphasize something. Filling out these forms is not the goal. Understanding the answers to these questions and using that information to maximize your effectiveness so you can improve sales velocity and predictability is the goal! Reviewing your opportunities and planning your activities will help you accomplish so much more at every meeting or during every phone call that you'll actually feel like you have *more* time.

You can't carry this much information about eight or ten different accounts around in your head. Use these sheets—or some electronic equivalent—to help manage all that data. Tools like these planning sheets will help you leverage your time and effort so you can manage more opportunities at one time. If you take the time to capture this information, you can share it with your manager or other members

Precall Planning Sheet

Date: _____

Account: _____   Opportunity: _____

Who are we meeting with or speaking to?

Name(s), title(s), and responsibility(ies)?

Who do they report to both directly and indirectly?

What role(s) do they play in the evaluation, approval, or purchasing process?

Which aspect(s) of *why* they would buy do we need to learn more about?
(Current state, desired future state, any of the six action drivers, or their vision of the ideal solution)

Which aspect(s) of *how* they would buy do we need to learn more about?
Refer to 11-20 on the opportunity scorecard or whatever is missing from the customer results plan.

What are we trying to accomplish?

What is the purpose of this meeting or call?

What is the ideal outcome?

What do we need our customer to agree to or commit to?

What specific step do we want our customer to take during or after the meeting?

What, specifically, do we need to communicate to them at this meeting?

What else needs to happen at this meeting?

Who else do we need them to introduce us to or agree to let us meet with?

Available at: **Sales Excellence.com**

Figure 6.7 Precall Planning Sheet

of your sales team so they can be more effective in helping you strategize and plan your sales efforts.

Keep Your Opportunities Moving

To accelerate your customer's buying process and maximize sales velocity, you have to keep your sales opportunities moving. Take a minute to think about the best opportunity in your sales portfolio. Is that opportunity moving or stopped? Here's how to tell the difference: If you have an appointment on your calendar to meet or speak with someone in that account—and if they have the appointment on their calendar too—then the opportunity is moving. If your customer doesn't have an appointment to meet or speak with you on their calendar, then the opportunity is stopped.

When a meeting or phone call has gone well, it's very tempting to wrap it up by saying, "Thanks for meeting with me. I'll give you a call next week." The problem is that when you call them in a week, you will probably end up playing phone tag for another week. When you finally do get them on the phone, it's likely that you'll book your next appointment for the following week. By then *three weeks* will have gone by! You will have lost any momentum that you might have created.

Sometimes, it's even worse. If your customer was just being polite in your first meeting and doesn't really want to meet with you again, it could take you two or three weeks of chasing them to find that out. Meanwhile, you've been emotionally invested in the opportunity for all that time when you could have used that energy to find or work on some other opportunity.

Your number one goal for every meeting or phone call should be to book the next meeting or phone call. This one simple step will help you qualify the opportunity to make sure your prospect really does want to meet with you again.

Go into every meeting knowing exactly what you will ask your prospect to do next if the meeting goes well. Then book that next appointment before you leave. By keeping your opportunities moving, you will ensure that you are investing your time and efforts wisely. You'll also cut time out of your overall sales cycle and maximize sales velocity.

* * *

I am often asked, "This seems like a lot of work to do for every single account. Do you really have to do all of this to structure each and every opportunity?" The answer, of course, is no. If you properly qualify the opportunities in your pipeline, you will determine that some of them don't warrant this kind of effort—at least not at this point. Invest your time in structuring the larger opportunities that have a high probability of actually coming to closure. But even when working the smaller opportunities in your portfolio, every one of the techniques and approaches here will make you far more effective.

You may not choose to construct a complete customer results plan for every opportunity, but you should at least seek to frame each opportunity so you can estimate when it is likely to close. You should also seek to understand the stages and steps involved in the customer's buying process and who will be involved in those various stages and steps so you can stay aligned with your customer and sell to as many of the right people as you can.

You may not sit down and complete an opportunity review and a precall plan for every meeting or phone call, but you should at least think about what you have learned about the opportunity thus far, and what else you need to learn going forward. If you choose not to complete the various templates and worksheets for each opportunity, you should at least use them as a reference and review them frequently to make sure you are not forgetting important steps along the way.

I recommend utilizing these concepts and tools in proportion to the size and importance of each opportunity. It ultimately becomes a matter of time management. Only you (or you and your manager) can decide how best to invest your time. But if you are working on a sizable opportunity—one that involves multiple influencers and approvers and which could take several months to close—it's worth investing whatever time is required to properly structure and manage the process for maximum results.

CHAPTER SEVEN

Selling Financial Results to Senior Executives

The results-based selling method is heavily focused on understanding your customer's goals and objectives so you can position your solutions to help them achieve their desired business results. In order to facilitate business-level discussions with your customers—and especially the executives involved in a buying decision—you have to be able to communicate how the capabilities of your products and services can help them improve some aspect of their business.

In this chapter, we explore the way executives think—and what they think *about*—based on the responsibilities of the positions they hold. We look closely at how companies measure their results and what impact your solutions could have on their financial performance. Then, we talk about how to connect the dots between your capabilities and your customer's goals and objectives so you can translate the value of what you sell into measurable business results.

Engaging Senior-Level Executives

Selling to senior executives, especially those at the C-level (CEO, COO, CFO, CIO, etc.), requires a very different approach from selling to Clem or his manager, Joe. You can sometimes catch Clem's interest by talking about the superiority of your technology or how much easier his life would be if he was using your service. But if there are any executives involved in the evaluation, selection, and approval process, they will be focused on the tangible and measurable business results they can produce by using what you sell. Therefore, the results-based selling approach is absolutely essential.

The broadcast approach, which we talk about in Chapter Two, simply doesn't work with executives for a couple of reasons. One is that they don't have time to listen. They have so many responsibilities and so many people to interface with that listening to a deluge of everything your product does feels like a waste of time to them.

The second reason is that—in many cases—executives don't have the technical knowledge to understand all the features and functions of your product anyway. If you want an executive to have an interest in what you sell, you have to translate the functional capabilities of your products and services into the measurable business results that they understand and care about.

What Executives Think About

Even if you've never held the position of CEO, you can teach yourself to think like a CEO by learning to think *about* what CEOs and other senior executives think *about*. Figure 7.1 shows a sample of some of the top of mind issues for most senior executives.

Profitability (or earnings) is one of the primary concerns of most senior executives because earning a profit is the ultimate financial objective of every for-profit company. Executives are also very concerned with consistent and predictable growth and the performance of their company's stock. Not only is it their job to profitably grow the company and produce a favorable return for their shareholders,

What Executives Think About

Earnings

Total revenues minus total costs and expenses. Often referred to as net profit or the *bottom line*. When divided among all outstanding shares of common stock, it is referred to as earnings per share (EPS).

Growth

Achieving consistent and predictable increases in sales revenue through organic growth (i.e., selling more through existing infrastructure) or through strategic mergers and acquisitions.

Stock Performance

Achieving consistent and predictable growth in the value (price) of each share of stock which meets analyst and investor expectations. This reduces shareholder turnover and leads to greater demand for each share of stock.

Market Share

A company's sales revenue within a particular market divided by the total sales revenue available in that market. Growing market share results in increased sales revenue and greater competitive strength.

Strategic Advantage

Any advantage a company may possess that makes them more competitive and is impossible or extremely difficult for their competitors to duplicate. This could include faster time to market, higher quality products, lower operating costs, better customer service, etc.

Quality

Reducing product defects or eliminating mistakes and errors in all facets of business operations. Initiatives such as Total Quality Management (TQM) or Six Sigma drive quality improvements which result in increased profitability.

Asset Management

Creating the greatest possible revenue and profit with the smallest amount of employed assets resulting in better return on assets (ROA) and return on invested capital (ROIC). Doing more with less investment and infrastructure.

Risk Management

The practice of eliminating, avoiding, or reducing the negative effects (consequences) of the risks involved in managing a business enterprise.

Regulatory Compliance

Maintaining compliance with legislation and government regulations that affect how a company operates, finances, manages, or markets their business.

Corporate Image and Culture

The image and culture a company fosters which attracts and retains customers, shareholders, employees, and business partners. The right corporate culture can also improve safety, quality, and productivity, which leads to profitability.

Available at: **SalesExcellence.com**

Figure 7.1 What Executives Think About

but many executives' compensation and bonuses are tied to measures like EPS (earnings per share) and stock performance. Therefore, the ways in which your clients can use your solutions to increase revenues (to drive growth) or reduce costs and expenses (to improve profitability) are almost always good topics for discussion.

Other popular subjects for executive-level conversations are how your solutions can be used to improve the quality of *their* products and services, get more productivity or greater return on investment from their existing assets, or mitigate any downside risks that could have a negative impact on their business.

Executives in certain industries such as pharmaceuticals, energy, health care, communications, and others are concerned with regulatory compliance and pending legislation. Executives in every industry are always concerned with improving their public image and corporate culture. Put simply, executives are concerned with the issues that have the potential to substantially impact business operations and performance.

Executive Roles and Responsibilities

Depending on their job title and position with their company, each executive has different responsibilities. Thus, each one will have a different set of goals and objectives, as well as a unique set of business problems they have to deal with. There is no way to know exactly what any particular executive is focused on until you meet them and engage them in a conversation. But you should learn the most common concerns of the role of each executive you will likely be selling to so that you can be prepared to position your solutions to solve specific problems or deliver specific results.

Figure 7.2 shows a few of the most important objectives for seven senior executive roles in a typical high-tech manufacturing company.

Executive Roles and Responsibilities
High-Tech Manufacturer

Chief Executive (CEO, President, Managing Director, Managing Partner)
- ▲ Earnings (EPS) or Net Profit
- ▲ Revenue Growth
- ▲ Stock Performance
- ▲ Market Share
- ▲ Corporate Image
- ▲ Competitive Strategy
- ▲ Business Planning
- ▲ Corporate Culture

Financial Executive (CFO, Treasurer, Finance Director, VP of Finance)
- ▲ Financial Position
- ▲ Return on Invested Capital
- ▲ Asset Management
- ▲ Cash Flow (Cash Management)
- ▼ Indirect Labor Costs
- ▲ Regulatory Compliance
- ▲ Investment Diversification
- ▲ Risk Management

Operations Executive (COO, President, Operations Director, VP of Ops.)
- ▲ Operating Profit
- ▲ On-Time Deliveries
- ▲ Workforce Productivity
- ▼ Direct Labor Costs
- ▼ Inventory Levels
- ▲ Regulatory Compliance
- ▲ Workplace Safety
- ▼ Cost of Materials (Goods)

Research and Development Executive (CTO, VP of R&D, VP of Eng.)
- ▲ Product Innovation
- ▼ Time to Market
- ▲ Product Quality
- ▲ Customer Satisfaction
- ▲ Product Reliability
- ▲ Product Safety
- ▲ Design Collaboration
- ▲ Regulatory Compliance

Sales and Marketing Executive (CSO, CMO, Sr. VP of Sales and Mktg.)
- ▲ Gross Revenue
- ▲ Gross [Profit] Margins
- ▲ Sales Forecast Accuracy
- ▼ Cost of Sales
- ▲ Market Share
- ▲ Brand Recognition
- ▲ Customer Loyalty
- ▲ Advertising ROI

Human Resources Executive (Exec. VP of Human Resources, VP of HR)
- ▲ Corporate Culture
- ▲ Workforce Productivity
- ▲ Compensation Strategy
- ▲ Employee Satisfaction
- ▼ Training and Dev. Costs
- ▲ Employee Retention
- ▲ Succession Planning
- ▲ Regulatory Compliance

Information Technology Executive (CIO, Sr. VP of IT, VP of IT)
- ▲ User Community Satisfaction
- ▲ Infrastructure Integrity
- ▲ Systems Integration
- ▲ Systems and Data Security
- ▲ Data Availailability
- ▲ Service Levels (Uptime)
- ▲ Disaster Recovery Prep.
- ▼ Operating and Maint. Costs

Available at: **Sales**Excellence.com

Figure 7.2 Executive Roles and Responsibilities

The ▲ next to some areas of responsibility suggests that most companies would most likely want to increase, improve, maximize, or have more of that business result. The ▼ means they would probably rather decrease, reduce, shorten, minimize, or have less of it. As you read through each description, think about how your company and the products and services you sell can impact each one.

Executive titles vary widely across industries. Hospitals often call their chief executive the hospital administrator. Large retailers have a vice president of merchandising, who is responsible for product selection, sourcing, negotiation, and pricing. Some financial services firms have a chief lending officer responsible for the segment of their business that loans money to borrowers. Start by determining the various executives within the industries that you sell to who might play a role in the decision to buy what you sell. Then learn all you can about the responsibilities involved in each role.

When you sell to smaller companies, the executives you deal with will probably have a broader base of responsibilities and concerns. You might find a business owner, a president, or a vice president who runs the entire company. Once you understand their roles and responsibilities, you can learn how to position your products and services to help them achieve the goals and objectives they are responsible for achieving.

The Language of the Senior Executive

The language used by high-level business managers and executives is usually quite different from the language used in IT, R&D, or out on the shop floor. To be effective selling to all the different people involved in a complex buying process, you have to become multilingual. In my workshops, I often invite an executive from my client's organization to say a few words and answer questions from the participants.

One CFO put it best when he told his sales team, "When you meet with senior executives, you have to explain what your solutions can do for them in terms they can understand. I sometimes attend meetings with salespeople from other companies who are trying to sell to us. If all they talk about are the features and functions of their products, it's a total waste of my time. When they start assuming that I understand all the technical lingo and acronyms they are throwing around, I start looking for a graceful way to leave."

If you wanted to learn to speak French, you could start by reading a book or listening to a tape or a CD. But if you really wanted to become fluent, you would need to associate with people who speak French. The only way to become fluent in the language of business is to immerse yourself in the culture and the environment.

You could hardly be considered credible and competent as a medical advisor or a law consultant if you were not fluent in the terminology of medicine or law. Business, too, has a language all its own, and each vertical industry has its own dialect. You don't have to become a CPA to be able to sell business results, but you will need to be able to converse with executives and have meaningful discussions in *their* language. This language is not only dollars and cents. It includes terms, measures, and metrics such as faster time to market, greater competitive advantage, better return on assets, etc.

The best way to start learning the language is to make a habit of reading the things executives read. *The Wall Street Journal, Business-Week, Fortune,* and *Forbes* are all good places to start. There may also be trade journals or other publications that are specific to the industry or market your customer competes in that could be a great resource.

To learn the specific vocabulary of your target prospect, read their annual report or their Form 10-K, which all publicly traded companies are required to submit to the SEC. Most companies make these readily available on their Web sites. You will find these materials filled with financial reports that can be a little overwhelming at first. But learning to read and understand these kinds of documents is an important part of becoming effective at selling to the executive level.

Selling Financial Results

Because of the broad variety of measures and metrics that businesses use to track and report their performance, learning the language of business is an ongoing process. If you sell across multiple industries— such as manufacturing, financial services, retail, and health care—it will take a while to learn all the terms and jargon used by executives within each industry. Fortunately, there is one universal standard for measuring business performance that applies to every for-profit company: Executives all over the world measure their business in terms of financial results.

While many businesses use a unique set of KPIs (key performance indicators) or success metrics to measure and manage the various aspects of their business, there is one set of business performance "scorecards" that are basically universal. These are called financial statements. The three major financial statements companies use are the *income statement*, the *balance sheet*, and the *statement of cash flows*.

Governments and other regulatory bodies all over the world require publicly traded companies to produce and disclose these financial statements for the benefit of current or prospective shareholders. Financial statements are also used internally by executives to monitor their company's progress and to support informed decisions about how to make their businesses more competitive, more profitable, and more attractive to potential investors.

Executives know that any purchase or investment they choose to make will ultimately have an impact on one or more of their financial statements. A small investment will usually have only a small impact.

But if what you sell costs hundreds of thousands of dollars—and the potential payback over the useful life of your product or service is in the millions—the impact could be enormous. It only makes sense that if executives think about how the purchase of your products or services will impact their financial results, you should too!

Impacting the Income Statement

The income statement, which is often referred to as a *profit and loss statement* (P&L), records all the income generated and all the costs and expenses incurred by a company during a given fiscal period (month, quarter, or year). Whatever is left over after subtracting all expenses from all income is considered net profit or the *bottom line*. This financial report measures business performance and the effectiveness of the executives who manage it.

Although the basic structure of an income statement is fairly standard, the way companies choose to categorize their income and expenses varies widely from industry to industry. A large financial services firm might categorize income into interest from loans, insurance premiums, and commissions, while a pharmaceuticals firm lumps all income together and calls it revenue. A restaurant chain could categorize operational expenses by food costs, occupancy costs, and payroll, whereas a high-tech manufacturer would break down expenses by research and development, sales and marketing, and administrative costs.

To make the most of this discussion, print or download the most recent income statement for a few of your prospective clients to get a better feel for how the companies that you want to sell to record revenue and expenses. Figure 7.3 shows a somewhat generic example of an income statement complete with the math behind the numbers and a definition for each line item.

The objective is to learn exactly how your products and services can be used to have a positive impact on one or more of the line items on your customer's income statement. You should think about:

- How can your customer use your products to increase their income?
- How do your services help your clients reduce costs or expenses?
- What impact can your solutions have on your customer's bottom line?

Answering questions like these and learning to share the answers with your clients is how you begin selling the value of financial results.

Impacting the Balance Sheet

The balance sheet, which is sometimes called a *statement of financial position,* is used to report everything that a company owns (its assets) minus everything the company owes (its liabilities). The balance remaining after they subtract liabilities from assets is recorded as *shareholders' equity.* Here again, assets and liabilities are categorized in a way that is meaningful for the type of company issuing the report.

Download or print the balance sheet for a few of the companies represented in your active opportunity portfolio and compare it to the generic example of a balance sheet in Figure 7.4. Become familiar with the way the companies you sell to categorize their assets and their liabilities. Then learn exactly how your solutions can have a positive impact on their balance sheet.

If your prospective client carries inventories, how could the client use your solutions to reduce inventories and free up cash for reinvestment? If one of your customers sells on credit and therefore has accounts receivable, can you and your company do anything to help them shorten their receivables cycle or reduce bad debt and improve their cash flow?

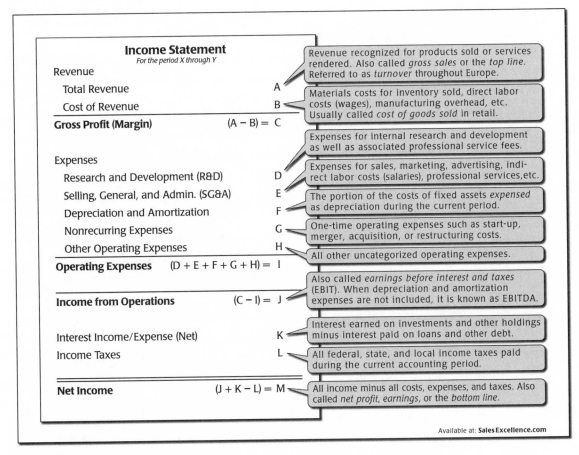

Figure 7.3 Sample Income Statement

The balance sheet is a little more complicated than the income statement in that it is not always obvious which line items your customer wants more of and which ones they want less of. An increase in accounts receivable could be good; it increases current assets and could suggest a marked increase in sales. But if accounts receivable are increased because customers aren't paying their bills on time, it could be an early indicator of cash flow problems.

You don't have to become a financial expert, but you will have to be able to articulate the benefits of using your product or service in terms of dollars and cents. To start with, learn which lines on these two financial statements you and your solutions can have an impact on. Later in this chapter we talk about exactly how to do that.

Selling Return on Investment

One of the ways that executives estimate or measure the financial impact of a specific project or investment is by considering its return on investment (ROI). A *forward-looking* ROI projection can be used to estimate the potential return and justify an investment in your solution. Companies often compare the ROI of multiple projects or initiatives to decide which ones are the best use of limited capital dollars. In this way, we sometimes have to compete for capital with a variety of projects or investments; therefore helping your customer create a compelling ROI can be a vital step in bringing an opportunity to closure.

Companies sometimes use a *backward-looking* ROI study to evaluate the actual return on a particular purchase or project. This can also be a valuable exercise in proving to your customer (and to yourself) that the investment ultimately did produce a favorable return. Assuming they are willing to let you share the information, this can be a great tool for making future sales to other customers.

Learning to use ROI as part of a sales strategy can be uncomfortable for salespeople if they don't have a background in finance. But it doesn't have to be this way. The basic premise of ROI is quite simple. An ROI is simply a record of cash inflows (return) and cash outflows (investment) over a given period of time. The confusing part is how any particular company defines and calculates both return and investment.

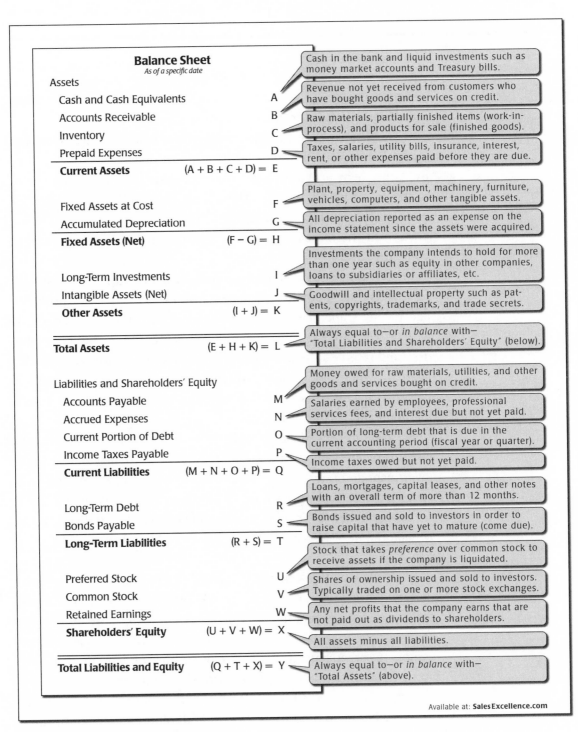

Balance Sheet
As of a specific date

Assets

Cash and Cash Equivalents	A	Cash in the bank and liquid investments such as money market accounts and Treasury bills.
Accounts Receivable	B	Revenue not yet received from customers who have bought goods and services on credit.
Inventory	C	Raw materials, partially finished items (work-in-process), and products for sale (finished goods).
Prepaid Expenses	D	Taxes, salaries, utility bills, insurance, interest, rent, or other expenses paid before they are due.
Current Assets	(A + B + C + D) = E	

Fixed Assets at Cost	F	Plant, property, equipment, machinery, furniture, vehicles, computers, and other tangible assets.
Accumulated Depreciation	G	All depreciation reported as an expense on the income statement since the assets were acquired.
Fixed Assets (Net)	(F − G) = H	

Long-Term Investments	I	Investments the company intends to hold for more than one year such as equity in other companies, loans to subsidiaries or affiliates, etc.
Intangible Assets (Net)	J	Goodwill and intellectual property such as patents, copyrights, trademarks, and trade secrets.
Other Assets	(I + J) = K	

Total Assets	(E + H + K) = L	Always equal to—or *in balance* with— "Total Liabilities and Shareholders' Equity" (below).

Liabilities and Shareholders' Equity

Accounts Payable	M	Money owed for raw materials, utilities, and other goods and services bought on credit.
Accrued Expenses	N	Salaries earned by employees, professional services fees, and interest due but not yet paid.
Current Portion of Debt	O	Portion of long-term debt that is due in the current accounting period (fiscal year or quarter).
Income Taxes Payable	P	Income taxes owed but not yet paid.
Current Liabilities	(M + N + O + P) = Q	

Long-Term Debt	R	Loans, mortgages, capital leases, and other notes with an overall term of more than 12 months.
Bonds Payable	S	Bonds issued and sold to investors in order to raise capital that have yet to mature (come due).
Long-Term Liabilities	(R + S) = T	

Preferred Stock	U	Stock that takes *preference* over common stock to receive assets if the company is liquidated.
Common Stock	V	Shares of ownership issued and sold to investors. Typically traded on one or more stock exchanges.
Retained Earnings	W	Any net profits that the company earns that are not paid out as dividends to shareholders.
Shareholders' Equity	(U + V + W) = X	All assets minus all liabilities.

Total Liabilities and Equity	(Q + T + X) = Y	Always equal to—or *in balance* with— "Total Assets" (above).

Figure 7.4 Sample Balance Sheet

As an example, if you sell a client $300,000 worth of CRM (customer relationship management) software, and during the first year of using it they increase their sales by $3 million, does that mean they saw a 1,000 percent ROI in just one year? Not necessarily. Your client probably can't attribute that entire increase in sales to the use of your software. There were many different factors that went into achieving those results. They could only say that some portion of the increase in sales was a return on the investment in your software.

In this scenario, the money your client paid you for the software represents only a portion of their overall investment. They probably had to buy some new computer equipment to run it on. They had to pay software maintenance fees so they could access your help desk and receive software updates. They had to pay to have it implemented, which might have involved customization and integration with existing systems. Plus they had to train the people who would maintain and use the system.

We can only produce a credible ROI if we know exactly how our customer defines—and what they choose to include in—both investment and return. Therefore, it has to be a joint effort with your customer. Any ROI that we try to develop on our own may include returns that they don't think are possible or that they feel should not be factored in. It also may not include everything they consider as an investment.

While we may think that saving our client's salespeople 30 minutes of paperwork each day equates to $4,000 of additional sales made, their sales management might think it equates to 30 more minutes for the salespeople to play solitaire on the computer. Likewise, we may assume that they have the cash to pay for our software in their bank account, but they might decide to borrow the money at 8 percent interest, which makes the total investment that much greater. A solid ROI has to be based on their perception of both return and investment.

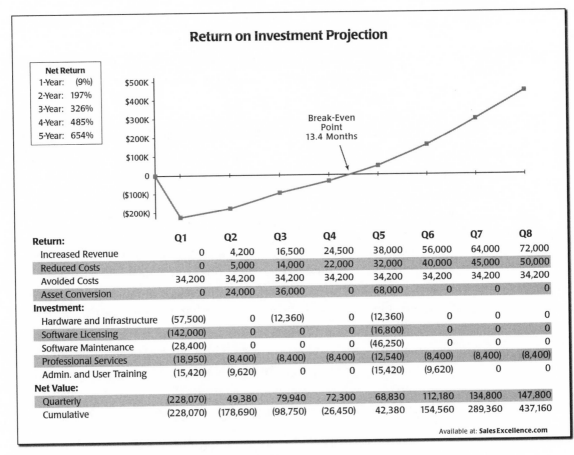

Figure 7.5 Sample Return on Investment Projection

Figure 7.5 shows an example of an ROI projection that breaks return into:

- *Increased revenue:* Whatever portion of additional sales your customer is willing to attribute to the success of this project.
- *Reduced costs:* Those reductions to costs your customer already incurs that are attributable to this investment.

- *Avoided costs:* Those costs that your customer won't have to incur as a result of this investment.
- *Asset conversion:* Any additional cash flow produced by this investment such as converting inventories or accounts receivable to cash.

This sample ROI shows investment categorized as in the previous CRM software example. The cash inflows and outflows are projected for each fiscal quarter over a two-year period, and the net value of the investment (either positive or negative) is shown at the bottom—both quarterly and on a cumulative basis. The line graph visually illustrates the cumulative net value of the investment.

This example is only one way to construct an ROI. The possible variations are endless. You may choose to create a standard template or an ROI calculator into which you can plug your client's numbers to produce some rough estimates. But if you determine that your customer will need to produce a more detailed ROI as part of the overall buying process, it is best to work with your customer using whatever format or templates that are used within their company.

Start by finding out how important ROI will be in your customer's buying decision. Try using hypothetical questions, such as:

- If you did decide you wanted to move forward with this project, how would you go about justifying the investment?
- Suppose you did get the support you needed from your executive manager. Would you or someone else have to produce an ROI projection to get financial approval?

You might also add a few open-ended questions to learn more about the process of obtaining funding, such as:

- How does your finance department decide which projects offer the greatest return on investment and the lowest element of risk?

Always begin by trying to learn how ROI is used to evaluate and justify investments and purchases at your client's company, rather than producing an ROI on their behalf. Any kind of ROI that you prepare without their involvement, or present to them in some format that they don't recognize, can actually work against you. Executives are usually very skeptical about vendors' claims of ROI. You can seriously damage your credibility if you present an ROI that doesn't include all the elements that they would consider part of the overall investment or that includes elements of return which they don't think should be included.

Using ROI effectively in a sales cycle will take learning how your client measures their business performance. You'll have to learn the metrics and the terminology they use internally to evaluate the viability of projects and investments. But when you communicate the value you can help bring to their business using their language, you'll be selling financial results instead of products and services.

Translating Capabilities into Financial Results

Selling financial results requires the sales professional to translate the functional capabilities of what a product or service can do into measurable business outcomes. This requires developing your business acumen (i.e., your understanding of how business works). To help salespeople learn how to translate capabilities into results, I have developed two very useful tools that accelerate the acquisition of business acumen: the capabilities and results sheet and the customer results map.

The Capabilities and Results Sheet

Translating business value means explaining exactly how your product or service impacts each executive involved in your customer's buying process. One tool that salespeople can use to translate capabilities into results is what I call a capabilities and results sheet. Figure 7.6 shows an example of what a sheet of this kind might look like for an inventory management system.

The left-hand column describes the functional capabilities of your product or service. This is not a list of features and functions; it's a description of what your product enables your customer to *do*. It might also include a very brief explanation of how your product makes that possible. The middle column describes the business results your customer can achieve by using your product. The right-hand column translates those results into the specific business impact on the various departments within your client's company.

This example shows the impact that an inventory management system can have on sales and marketing, operations, and finance. In my workshops, we use this tool in a small group exercise to help participants begin to think more in terms of customer outcomes, business results, and financial impact. Many of my clients adopt this concept to create materials for teaching their salespeople how to talk about new products and new technologies in business terms.

When this kind of information is made available and included in the product training that salespeople receive, they become much more comfortable and effective selling to senior-level executives. It promotes business conversations instead of sales presentations. Using tools like the capabilities and results sheet helps salespeople develop the business acumen and industry knowledge that is so critical in a complex selling environment.

The Customer Results Map

Depending on the vertical markets or industries you sell to, there are similarities in many of the business results that companies within

Capabilities and Results Sheet

Our Capabilities	Customer Results	Business Impact
Improve visibility of inventory levels across the enterprise: Our system provides real-time inventory status reporting that consolidates inventory information from all plants and distribution centers. The system combines data from multiple disparate data sources across and beyond the enterprise including inventory data from both suppliers and customers.	**Better balance supply and demand:** By having real-time, global visibility to inventories, companies can optimize inventory levels, balance supply with demand, improve operational efficiencies, and maximize profitability.	**Sales and Marketing:** Sales and Customer Service can provide their customers with more accurate delivery promises which reduces back orders and improves customer satisfaction ratings.
		Operations: Global visibility to inventory levels enables Operations and Manufacturing to do more accurate production planning, which leads to more accurate staff scheduling. This reduces redundant inventories and overruns that result in obsolete goods. It also improves utilization of manufacturing and warehouse space.
		Finance: Eliminating excessive raw materials, work in process, or finished goods inventories frees up cash for reinvestment (i.e., improves cash flow), improves a company's overall financial position, and has a positive impact on other key measures such as return on assets (ROA). It also eliminates carrying costs and expenses such as storage, heat, air conditioning, taxes, and insurance on excessive inventories.

To make the most of this concept, develop a capabilities and results sheet for all your major products. List each functional capability and translate that capability into customer results and measurable business impact.

Available at: **SalesExcellence.com**

Figure 7.6 Capabilities and Results Sheet

those industries are trying to achieve. Every high-tech manufacturer is focused on shortening time to market. Every telecommunications company is obsessed with customer retention. Every financial services firm is trying to grow their market share. The more you develop your knowledge of the business results you can help your clients achieve, the more effective you will be in using the results-based selling approach.

Another excellent tool for learning business acumen is what I call a customer results map. It is a visual depiction of your customer's business strategy that can be used to practice connecting the dots between the functional capabilities of your solutions and the achievement of your client's goals.

Please take a look at Figure 7.7. This is a visual representation of some of the goals, strategies, and tactical initiatives for a high-tech manufacturing company. Each vertical industry—in fact, every individual company—will have its own terminology for the various initiatives, measures, or metrics they use to track their business success. But this is a good example of the business strategy for a typical high-tech manufacturer.

At the very top of this model, you'll see the financial objective that every for-profit company wants to achieve: An increase in profit (earnings) that ultimately converts to greater equity or cash flows for the owners or shareholders. Just below that you'll see the three ways that a company can increase profits: Increase revenue (sell more), reduce costs (spend less), or better utilize their assets (do more with less). The first two relate primarily to the income statement, while the third relates more to the balance sheet. Most companies already have well-established goals in these three areas. All you have to do is articulate exactly how your products and services can help your customers achieve them.

Below the three primary goals are a number of different strategies and tactics that represent the various ways a high-tech manufacturer

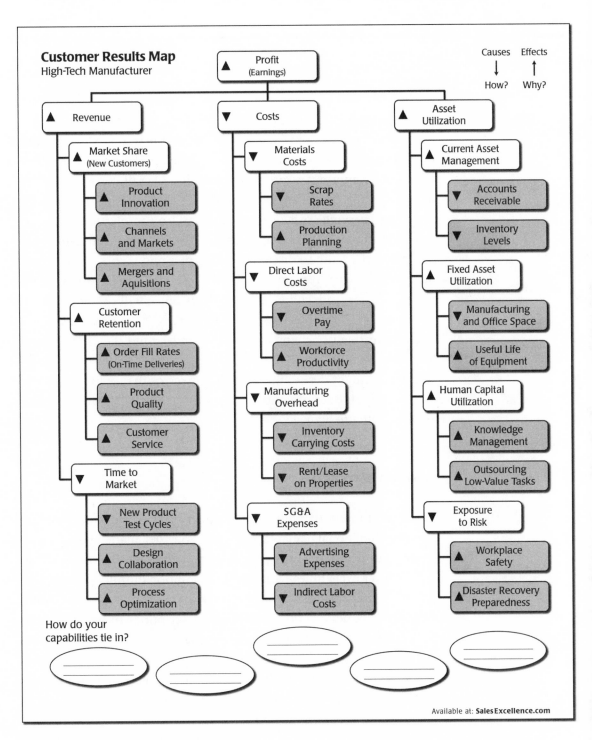

Figure 7.7 The Customer Results Map

might go about achieving those goals. One of the strategies for increasing revenue, for example, is increasing market share, while the various tactics for doing that might include better product innovation, additional channels or markets, and selected mergers and acquisitions An important strategy for reducing overall costs is reducing manufacturing overhead, which might be accomplished by reducing inventory carrying costs or rents and leases on properties.

The customer results map uses the same hierarchical cause-and-effect model we use to discuss the strategies and tactics of increasing our sales revenue in Chapter One. If you have attended one of my workshops, or read *Think Like Your Customer,* will recognize this as an extension of the Business Value Hierarchy™ concept. This model is very effective in helping salespeople understand the cause-and-effect relationships between all the different kinds of business results companies might desire. But the real power of the tool is using it to map the capabilities of your solutions to the goals that your client is already trying to achieve.

Solution Mapping

Think about one of your core products or services and its most valuable functional capabilities. Can you articulate one of those capabilities in a very short phrase, such as "global remote monitoring," "faster cycle times," or "higher resolution output"? Please note that it's not the name of your product we are looking for here—it's what the product can do. These short descriptions of product capabilities are easy to find within marketing literature and on product specification sheets.

If you were to write that brief description in one of the ovals at the bottom of the customer results map—and then draw a dotted line to the various tactical initiatives (in the gray boxes) that your capability could have an impact on—how many connections could you make?

There are dozens, if not hundreds, of different business initiatives that will result in increasing revenue, reducing costs, and improving asset utilization. Your product or service won't support them all. What you want to learn is, "What are the things that my prospective clients are already trying to do that my capabilities can help them do better, faster, cheaper, more reliably, with less hassle, with fewer mistakes, or using fewer people?" This is how you connect the dots between your capabilities and your customer's desired results.

If you don't know all the ways your solutions can be used to improve your customer's business, find someone who does. Go to your manager or someone else in your company who has a strong knowledge of the business issues your products and services can address and start to develop your own business acumen using the customer results map.

Because of the differences in the way companies within different industries measure and manage their business, I have created a number of different customer results maps for a variety of industries. In the appendix you will find examples including:

1. High-tech manufacturer
2. Consumer packaged goods (CPG) manufacturer
3. Communication services provider
4. Retailer
5. Financial services
6. Food service (Restaurant)
7. Pharmaceutical manufacturer
8. Not-for-profit healthcare (Hospital)

I encourage you to use these templates to practice explaining how the capabilities of your products and services tie in and support the achievement of your customer's most important goals. This will improve your ability to detect the gaps between your customer's current point A and their desired point C, and it will make you far more effective at positioning your B as the perfect fit.

If you spend the time to really get to know your customer's business, you can create a customer results map that is specific to their business. This can be a tremendous tool to facilitate business discussions and show how your capabilities tie to your customer's business objectives during executive-level presentations.

* * *

Selling to executives is challenging. It can even be intimidating, especially if you don't have a business management background. But you can learn to become comfortable with it if you immerse yourself in the right environment and are willing to make a few mistakes. You'll find that senior executives are some of the nicest people you will ever meet. They just have a lot of responsibilities and they are incredibly busy! If you will stay grounded in the results-based approach and think in terms of outcomes for your customers, you can become very effective at selling financial results to executives.

CHAPTER EIGHT

Delivering a Results-Based Sales Presentation

Depending on the environment you sell in, your job may involve delivering sales presentations to groups or individuals. Today, even salespeople who never leave their desk can present to audiences located anywhere in the world using a Web-conferencing solution or some other collaboration platform. Therefore, mastering the use of presentations to move opportunities forward, increase sales velocity, and improve your closure rate is an important skill for any sales professional.

In this chapter, we begin by examining the purpose of a presentation in the overall sales cycle. We look at what is required to prepare yourself and your audience before you present. We talk about the structure and content of an effective presentation, especially when presenting to senior executives. Then we discuss how to deliver your presentation and manage your meeting to maximize your results.

The Purpose of a Sales Presentation

Before we get into the specifics of presentation content and delivery, let's step back and think about the purpose of conducting a sales presentation to begin with. Like every other aspect of the results-based selling method, we need to understand what we are trying to accomplish and why we're trying to accomplish it before we put together our plan for how to do it.

Why Should We Use a Sales Presentation?

In Chapter Two, we talk about the concept I call selling with specific intent. The idea is that every step we take in our sales process should be done with the purpose of helping our customer take the next step they need to take in their buying process. Giving a presentation is no different. There could be a number of reasons for using a group presentation format. It could be used to:

- Facilitate a group discussion to define a shared vision of your customer's desired future state (C).
- Establish and promote organizational alignment among the various influencers and approvers.
- Present the findings from a needs analysis or opportunity assessment that you have conducted.
- Present an overview of your proposed solution to get group reaction and feedback.
- Demonstrate your proposed solution to a select group of approvers.
- Gain a consensus to move forward with your customer results plan.

Before you schedule a meeting with your client, always think about what you want to accomplish at the meeting. The opportunity review sheet we talk about in Chapter Six can help you establish where you are in the overall process, and the precall planning sheet will help you think about what you need to do next.

In one scenario, delivering a sales presentation to a group of approvers and influencers can be an excellent way to get buy-in for your proposed solution or to present your customer results plan. But in a different situation, a group presentation may not be the best "next step." It depends on where your customer is in their buying process and what you believe to be their next reasonable step.

When Should We Use a Sales Presentation?

Many salespeople are taught to give an introductory presentation at the first meeting with a new prospect in order to establish credibility. I disagree with this approach. If your customer didn't think you had something of value to offer, they probably wouldn't have agreed to meet with you in the first place.

The way you establish credibility is by having an interactive conversation about your customer's business. This gives you a chance to demonstrate your knowledge of their industry, your ability to diagnose business problems, and your creativity in crafting solutions that can help them achieve their desired business results. An introductory presentation that is all about you and your company is a classic example of the broadcast approach to selling.

Use your first meeting to ask questions, listen, and learn. You may need to share a little information about yourself and your company to create a two-way dialogue, but leave your laptop and projector in the car. If your client invites you to come and present to their selection committee at your first meeting, persuade them that you have no way of knowing *what* to present until you've had a chance to learn more about their business and the goals and objectives they are trying to accomplish.

Another common use of a sales presentation is to deliver a final proposal to a group of approvers and influencers. The problem with this approach is twofold. First, if you haven't had the opportunity to meet with all the different people that you will be presenting to, the chances that your proposal will hit the bull's-eye for each of them are pretty slim. Second, when one person starts pointing out what they don't like about your proposal, and the others decide to join in, the meeting can go downhill fast.

Instead of waiting until the end of a complex buying process to present to the group involved in making the decision, try to arrange an opportunity to present to them earlier in the overall process. We talk about the structure and content of that presentation a little later in this chapter. This will enable you to do two important things: One, it gives you a reason to meet each person before it's time to submit your final proposal so you can tailor the proposal to address more of their individual needs and concerns. Two, it may then be appropriate to submit your final proposal to a smaller group of senior people where it's easier to handle objections and work through any issues they may have.

Who Should We Be Presenting To?

If you've determined exactly what you want to accomplish with your presentation and decided that the timing is right, the next question is, "Who should we be presenting to?" Unfortunately, there is no simple answer. It all depends on what you want to accomplish with your presentation and what step it is designed to help your customer take next. What we do know, however, is that your customer can agree to take the next step only if the people responsible for making that kind of a commitment are present.

Think carefully about who you involve in your presentation—both from your company and from your customer's organization.

Having too many people from either company simply introduces more variables and makes the outcome that much less certain. Focus on the desired results for the meeting and the next reasonable step your customer needs to take. Then invite the people from your company and theirs that need to be there in order to make that happen.

Preparing for Your Presentation

The results-based selling philosophy is essential to crafting a presentation that will move your sales opportunity forward. Assuming you believe that a presentation is the appropriate next step to take in a particular opportunity, and you know who you need to present to, the next question is, "What do you want your audience to think differently or do differently after this presentation?"

As you plan your presentation, give some thought to the specific actions you want your customer to take after you are through. Do you want them to:

- Reach a consensus on their desired future state (C)?
- Agree on the need to move forward with a certain project?
- Confirm the findings of your needs analysis and approve your solution overview?
- Agree to move forward with your customer results plan?
- Commit to moving ahead with the purchase?

In essence, the question is, "What is your desired result?"

If you can define what you want your customer to think or do after the presentation is over, then you'll know what you need to communicate during the presentation to get the desired result. You can design your content and materials to accomplish that objective.

Selecting the Right Presentation Format

For many sales professionals, the word *presentation* has become synonymous with *slide show*. But using a laptop and a projector is *not* the only way to present to a group. There are a number of different formats or mediums that might be more appropriate for your next meeting.

Rather than setting up the projector, you could print your slides, hand them out, and talk through them as you and your audience sit around a conference table. This tends to promote much more group interaction and discussion than shutting off the lights and shining a picture on the wall.

Another very effective way to conduct a sales presentation is to prepare your content so it can be delivered as a "chalk talk" on a white board or a flip chart. This is particularly useful for doing impromptu meetings because it can be delivered without any props or equipment.

As you plan your next presentation, don't feel locked in to any particular technology or format. Remember that you have many options that might be better for facilitating discussion and making your presentation more interactive.

Meeting Your Audience before You Present

As you prepare yourself for an upcoming presentation, you should also do all you can to prepare your audience. It may not always be possible or feasible, but you should try to meet—or at least speak to—all the people you will be presenting to whenever you can. When presenting to a large group, talk to a representative sample of the group—especially those who will act as influencers and approvers in your customer's buying process.

Ask each person who will be attending about their role with the company, their expectations for the meeting, what they hope to get out of the presentation, or any concerns they would like you to address. Even a short telephone conversation will help to break down barriers and make each person you speak with more willing to actively participate in your meeting.

When appropriate, include information in your presentation that relates directly to the interests or concerns you heard during your preparation interviews. This makes your presentation more interesting and creates a much greater impact.

Establishing Shared Expectations

In order for your presentation to increase the velocity of your customer's buying process, always establish a shared definition of success and a clear plan to move forward. You'll need to properly set expectations for the meeting as well as what you and your customer will do after the meeting is over.

You can use hypothetical questions such as, "Assuming you are pleased with the solution overview and the implementation plan we present, will you be in a position to send your recommendation to your COO?" These kinds of questions are also very helpful in flushing out possible objections. Ask your customer, "If the meeting goes well, would there be any reason you wouldn't be ready or able to take the next step?" Make sure you and your customer know exactly what will happen next if the presentation is successful.

Crafting an Effective Executive-Level Presentation

If you apply the results-based selling approach, then every presentation you give will be unique based on who you are presenting to and what you want to accomplish. There are, however, certain types of presentations that you will conduct at some point in most every sales opportunity.

One example, which is an essential element of the results-based selling method, is an executive presentation that is delivered partway through your customer's buying process. This particular presentation is designed to accomplish several important objectives that we discuss later in this chapter. It is only one example of the many forms your presentations may take, but the components from which it is built have broad application and can be used in a variety of different ways.

The Right Time for an Executive-Level Presentation

When you find a new sales opportunity, you will most likely start by doing some general discovery to qualify the opportunity and determine if there is a fit for one or more of your solutions. You will hopefully meet several different people who will be involved in your customer's buying process, and—if you deem it appropriate—conduct some form of needs analysis or opportunity assessment.

At this point, you will hopefully have a good idea of your customer's current state (point A), their desired future state (point C), and the gap that exists between the two. Using the findings of your opportunity assessment, you will also have a good idea of how your products and services could be used to bridge the gap and help your customer achieve their desired business results.

If you have been given the opportunity to meet with the right people—and if you have used the approach of reverse-engineering discussed in Chapter Six—you'll also have some knowledge of their buying process as well as the steps that would be involved in implementing and using your solution to achieve their desired results.

This is an excellent time to request an opportunity to present to the key influencers and approvers involved in your customer's buying process so that you can evaluate organizational alignment and further qualify the opportunity. The players you most want at this presentation are the senior executives who will own the success of the project and the return on investment (the project owner and investment owner), as well as those who will provide financial approval, final approval, and ultimately sign your contract.

At this meeting you can provide what I refer to as a solution overview. This is a glimpse into your proposed solution but not a complete product demonstration. I recommend saving your full product demo for much later in the sales cycle. Whenever possible, your demonstration should simply be a proof of concept to show that you can actually do what you have said you can do. Ideally, all the approvers and influencers would have already agreed to move forward and place the order if your proof of concept is successful.

In the solution overview, you will focus on positioning your products and services as an ideal solution, explaining why you are the ideal partner to work with on this project, and introducing your proposed process (your customer results plan) for implementing and using your solution to accomplish their desired business results. You may also choose to discuss return on investment if you have been able to work with someone from their organization to create and validate an ROI projection.

The Executive Presentation Template

In my workshops, I introduce an executive presentation template, which provides the structure for an effective executive-level presentation to fit the scenario described above. Like everything else in the results-based selling method, this template is designed to achieve a specific result—namely to obtain or confirm executive-level buy-in to your customer results plan. The components of the executive presentation template are as follows:

1. Who we've met and what we've learned.
2. Confirmation of the customer's desired results (C).
3. How our solutions enable the achievement of our customer's goals.
4. A return on investment projection.
5. A case study of a reference client.
6. What makes us the ideal partner?
7. Our customer results plan.
8. The call to action.

Now let's take a closer look at each of these eight components:

1. Who We've Met and What We've Learned. To begin your executive presentation, start by reviewing who you have met with and what you have learned from them. This emphasizes your consultative, results-based approach. As you review what you have learned and seek confirmation from your audience, you may also discover that some things have recently changed. This will help you avoid presenting a solution based on bad or outdated information. Regardless of how much you try to meet everyone ahead of time, there might still be people at your presentation who you have never met. Reviewing what you have done so far will give you a chance to get everyone on the same page.

2. Confirmation of the Customer's Desired Results (C). Before you introduce any type of a solution, make sure you have an accurate understanding of your customer's collective point C. Each person in the room will have their own opinions, but this forum is an excellent place to understand how much consensus and organizational alignment does or does not exist.

If you find that some people in the room have a different vision of point C or that point C has shifted, spend your time ironing out the collective point C within the group. Presenting a B before you have clearly defined point C is always a bad move, even if you flew a thousand miles to deliver your presentation. Presenting a solution that does not match with their desired future state will hurt you far more than it will help.

3. How Our Solutions Enable the Achievement of Our Customer's Goals. Once you confirm point A and get a consensus on point C, then you are ready to share your solution to help them achieve those results. Here is where you will explain exactly how your solution ties to and supports each of your customer's major goals and objectives.

One good way to illustrate this is using a simplified version of the customer results map we discuss in Chapter Seven. Figure 8.1 shows two ways that you can show exactly how the functional capabilities of your solutions tie to your customer's desired business results.

Both of these are very effective presentation models. The first one, which features what I call the business value pyramid, shows how your solution and its functional capabilities tie to the tactical initiatives and strategies your customer will use to achieve a specific goal. The second one shows how one solution can actually support the achievement of multiple goals or objectives. These two models have broad application and are used in our workshops to help participants learn to connect the dots between their solutions and their client's goals.

4. A Return on Investment Projection. As we discuss in Chapter Seven, be careful about how you present any kind of ROI, payback analysis, or business case. Unless your ROI projection has been blessed by some high-ranking executive who is present at your meeting, you may cause a discussion that knocks your whole presentation off track.

ROI can be confusing for many of the people at your meeting because it can be calculated in so many different ways. If you have prepared an ROI that *has* been scrutinized and validated by your customer's financial people, it can be an extremely effective and compelling addition to your presentation. Just make sure you have someone from your client's company *in the room* who will support the validity of any ROI you choose to present.

5. A Case Study of a Reference Client. One question that you should expect your audience members to be asking themselves is, "Have these guys worked with any other companies like ours? Or are we the experiment?" Since you know this is likely to be a concern, include a case study or a reference story as part of your presentation. It doesn't have to be a company exactly like your prospective client, but the more similar it is, the more credibility the story will carry. If you can't find an existing client just like your new prospect, then at least find one who you have helped achieve some of the same business results that your new prospect wants to achieve.

6. What Makes Us the Ideal Partner? Finally, you get the chance to tell your prospective customer some things about your company and your people. But even here, position what makes you the ideal partner in relation to what you have learned about your customer's point C, not why you are so much better than your competitor. There will be differences in your company, your people, and your product and services solutions that set you apart. Help your customer appreciate how well your product or service fits with their vision of the ideal solution and why you are uniquely qualified to help them derive maximum business results.

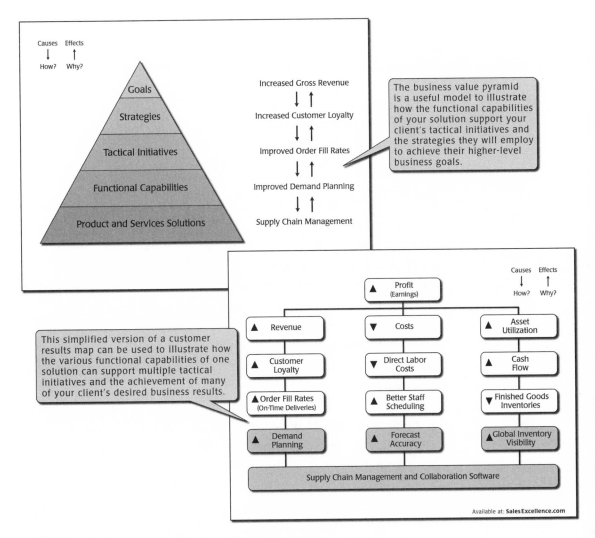

Figure 8.1 Tying Your Capabilities to Your Client's Goals

7. Our Customer Results Plan. Assuming that your customer likes what you've presented thus far and you feel it is appropriate to start talking about moving forward, you can present the customer results plan that you created with your client showing the action plan and the timeline to get them from where they are currently *all the way* to point C. Your goal is to obtain buy-in and acceptance of the plan from as many people in your customer's organization as you can. This often means you will make some changes to the plan right there in the meeting.

If your prospective customer decides to buy from you, they will be buying both your product *and* your plan of how they will use your product to achieve their desired results. That makes the customer results plan a critical part of your overall value proposition.

8. The Call to Action. At the end of your presentation, you'll want to issue a call to action as a way to close on the next reasonable step your customer needs to take. This may vary from one presentation to the next. In one case you might want the COO to buy in to your proposed customer results plan and confirm that the timeline is reasonable and accurate by asking, "Is there anything about the plan that we need to change, or are you ready to move forward with the next step?" This is a good example of the powerful either/or question structure and will tell you exactly where you stand with the opportunity.

In another scenario you might ask, "Is there any reason you wouldn't want to place the order today?" to try to close the deal right then and there. However you phrase it, the call to action is how you ask your customer to take—or commit to taking—the next step in their buying process and move the opportunity toward closure.

Fine-Tuning Your Presentation

Whether you use the executive presentation template or decide to structure your presentation differently, make sure that every slide or piece of information you include is in there for a reason. Look at each and every slide in your presentation deck and ask yourself, "What do

I want my audience to think differently or do differently after they see this slide?"

When I do consulting work with my clients who are preparing executive-level presentations, my rule of thumb is that if you can't explain exactly what purpose this particular slide is serving, then get it out of the deck! We don't have enough time as it is and our customers don't either. We certainly can't afford to waste any of it presenting things that don't serve a specific purpose. The fewer slides you have, the more time you will have to get your audience members involved in the discussion.

Presentation Delivery and Meeting Management

Once you've decided on your presentation format, prepared your audience, and put together your content, it's time to deliver your presentation. How you conduct your meeting and what you do to get your audience involved can make the difference between a presentation where everyone is cordial but unresponsive versus a meeting that accelerates your client's buying process and moves the opportunity forward.

Getting Your Venue Right

The venue or setting in which you present can have an enormous impact on the effectiveness of your presentation. A great setting won't make up for weak content or a sloppy delivery, but a serious problem with your setting can make an otherwise terrific presentation absolutely useless.

Make sure that your room is the right size for the group and that you've got the right number of chairs. If you have people standing at the back, they will almost certainly start talking and/or going in and out of the room. This can be a huge distraction for everyone else and is particularly embarrassing when your client's CEO is one of the people who has to stand.

Confirm that you have the room reserved for longer than you expect your meeting to run. Nothing ruins your presentation faster than another group showing up and demanding that you clear the room for their meeting. If you are using a projector, select a light slide background and dark text and graphics that can be seen and read well in a fully lit room. Turning off the lights puts your audience to sleep and dramatically reduces group interaction.

These might seem like little things that are almost too simplistic to mention. But any one of these "little things" can render a presentation that was designed to close a million dollar sale completely ineffective.

Setting the Meeting Parameters

As you open your meeting, take a minute to go over your agenda and make sure you and your audience have the right expectations. If you need to change something or someone needs to leave before you had planned to end, handle those adjustments right then. Don't get half-way through your one-hour presentation before you find out that a third of your audience has to leave after the first 45 minutes. Review your shared definition of success, and—if appropriate—the next step you will be proposing if the meeting goes as planned.

You may choose to bring in an expert to participate in your presentation, such as a technical specialist who will demonstrate your product or an executive from your company. But it is important for you (the account executive or sales representative) to open, close, and assume responsibility for the meeting. Establishing the proper expectations will make your presentation and your meeting go more smoothly and ensures that you accomplish your desired results.

Connecting with Your Audience

As you start your meeting, take the time to go around the room and have each person give their name and express what they would like to take away from today's meeting. You might hear something new that will influence your presentation or discussion. Remember, you're not there to blindly present a set of prepared slides. With any luck, you'll get some audience input that will help you shape your presentation to make it even more relevant and effective.

Exchanging even a few words with each person in the room creates a connection that will make them feel more comfortable adding a comment or asking a question later on. It also gives you license to request input or direct a question specifically to them. The value of this step cannot be overemphasized. This will make a huge difference in how comfortable your audience members will be with getting actively involved in the meeting.

Getting Your Audience Involved

As you work through your presentation, get confirmation that your audience understands what you are presenting. If you wait until the end of a 60-minute presentation to ask, "Are there any questions?" you may find that you lost most of them early on.

Ask general questions directed toward the group and solicit input and feedback from each person if you can. Anytime you direct a question to a specific person, you run the risk of putting them on the spot, but the risk of *not* getting your audience involved and engaged is far greater.

A presentation without audience interaction is just as ineffective as using the broadcast approach to selling. Do your best to get each person in the room to express their thoughts, offer input, ask questions, or provide feedback on what you are presenting.

Staying on Schedule

One of the most important elements of a successful meeting is managing your time properly, especially starting and ending on time. If your presentation starts running behind, you may not accomplish your desired results before your participants have to run to their next scheduled meeting. Make sure you build time into your presentation to get your audience involved in the discussion. Your objective is to cause some specific shift in thinking and behavior—not to get through all of your slides.

Even the best planned presentation can get off track if you allow the group to get bogged down discussing some trivial ancillary matter. One good technique is to use what is often referred to as a "parking lot." This is a flip chart or other mechanism to capture ideas or action items to be taken up after the meeting is over. Being able to place an action item in the parking lot so you can come back to it later helps you keep the meeting on schedule.

When you come to the end of your allotted time, don't start rushing through your material or asking people to stay longer. A few people might not care. But for others, it could be a major inconvenience. You would be better off stopping the presentation and scheduling a follow-up meeting. Budget your time carefully and stay focused on your desired outcomes and results.

Wrapping Up Your Meeting

To keep your sales opportunities moving, you need to schedule your next appointment at the end of every meeting. This applies equally to group presentations. Carefully manage your time so you are finished presenting and have had time to either handle or "park" all questions and objections. Leave yourself a few minutes to review any action items you have accepted, as well as the action items your customer has committed to.

Scheduling the next step as you wrap up your presentation is actually the most important part of your meeting. You can skip any number of slides or totally forget to mention certain information, but if you wrap things up by scheduling your next appointment, you can always revisit it next time. Arranging your plans to move the opportunity forward is the most important result of any presentation.

* * *

In the final analysis, the success of a sales presentation is not measured by how much information you were able to convey or even how enthusiastic your audience was about what you presented. The value of a presentation is in moving the sales opportunity toward closure. As you prepare, as you deliver, and as you wrap up your meeting, stay focused on helping your customer take the next step they need to take in their buying process and move one step closer to their desired point C.

CHAPTER NINE

Closing and Negotiating for Maximum Results

Contrary to popular perception, closing and negotiating are not isolated events that happen only at the end of a sales cycle. They both happen during virtually every telephone call and during every meeting. When you call a new prospect and ask, "Can you speak now, or would you prefer I call you back at a specific time?" you are *closing* on, or arranging, a telephone conversation. When you work with your client to find the right date and time for your next meeting—as well as who will attend and what topics will be discussed—you are *negotiating* a next step that works for both parties.

In the results-based selling method, closing and negotiating skills are needed in every stage of the sales cycle. They are used in scheduling appointments, gaining access to senior executives, reaching an agreement on pricing and contract terms, and resolving customer issues before or after the sale. Therefore, a strong foundation in closing and negotiating is vital for anyone who interacts with customers.

In this chapter, we begin by looking at what negotiation is and what it isn't. We discuss how negotiation facilitates closure as you help your customer work through the steps of their buying process. We explore a systematic approach to closing and negotiating that can be used in a variety of different scenarios. Then we talk about applying the principles of effective negotiations in order to reduce price erosion and maximize your sales results.

What Negotiation Is and Isn't

At Sales Excellence, Inc., we receive many calls from prospective clients who want to train their salespeople to be better negotiators. Our first question is, "Why?" One application of negotiation skills, for example, is handling and overcoming objections, which can make working through the steps of your customer's buying process go more smoothly and shorten the length of your average sales cycle. Negotiation skills are also critical in reducing price erosion and improving profit margins when it comes time to negotiate pricing and contract terms. But surprisingly, the most common answer we hear is, "We are losing too many sales to our competitors." After a short discussion, we often find that this is an inaccurate diagnosis that stems from a misconception of what negotiation is and what it isn't.

Negotiating vs. Positioning

Once in a while, a breakdown in final pricing or contract negotiations can force a customer to abandon their vendor of choice and enter into negotiations with an alternate vendor. But many of the prospective clients we talk to—who feel they are losing too many sales to their competitors—are never being selected as the vendor of choice in the first place. There is a big difference between negotiating and positioning.

Your power, and thus your success, in negotiating final pricing and contract terms is determined by how well you have prepared and positioned yourself throughout the sales cycle. The earlier you start to set yourself apart from your competition, the more power you have when final price negotiations begin.

If your customer doesn't believe that your solution is a better fit or that it doesn't represent superior value over your competitor's offering, there's actually nothing to negotiate *about*. Differentiate *before* you negotiate. If you haven't successfully positioned yourself as the best choice in the mind of your customer, you actually lost the deal long before it came time to negotiate contract terms and pricing.

Negotiating vs. Bidding

We have all probably heard a prospective client say—either verbally or via a request for proposal (RFP)—"We are considering buying a certain quantity of a certain product with the following specifications. Please respond with the availability and your best price." Submitting a quote or proposal at the lowest possible profit margin in hopes of having the lowest price is not negotiating. That's bidding.

You may choose to submit a bid that represents a substantial discount from your list price, but in your customer's mind, that is the starting place. If you are selected as the vendor of choice, further negotiation often follows. Be careful not to give away all your profit margin in order to be the lowest bidder. You may need to leave yourself some room to negotiate even after you offer your "best price."

How Negotiation Facilitates Closure

In the results-based selling method, *closing* is not a dirty word. That is, unless your idea of closing is convincing or persuading your customer to do something they don't want to do or is not in their best interest. Put simply, closing is reaching an agreement or asking your customer to make a commitment to take the next step in their evaluation and buying process. That next step could be to meet with you on Thursday at two o'clock. Or it could be to sign a half-million-dollar contract. Closing or reaching agreement on each step we take with our customer is a very natural part of working together and helping them to reach their desired future state (point C).

Negotiation, on the other hand, is the way that you make the proposed next step agreeable and acceptable to both parties. This may involve some aspect of give-and-take or trade-off with your customer so that both parties feel that their interests are properly served. But negotiating is required only when the next step is *not* acceptable to either you or your customer *as proposed*. First, you try to close on the next reasonable step. Then, if necessary, you negotiate.

The Results-Based Negotiation Process

The skills involved in closing and negotiating are absolutely fundamental for any sales professional. That does not necessarily mean that they are simplistic, or that negotiating and closing sales opportunities is easy. Unless a salesperson has a system or a process for handling objections and conducting negotiations, bringing an opportunity to closure can be extremely difficult.

To help salespeople become more consistent and effective negotiators, I've developed what I call the results-based negotiation process, which is shown in Figure 9.1. It is a repeatable series of steps and actions that a salesperson can take to move sales opportunities forward.

This process can be used to negotiate and close on the next step in your customer's buying process, to negotiate final pricing and contract terms, or to overcome customer objections at any point in the overall

Results-Based Negotiation Process

Step 1: Ask Your Client to Take the Next Step (Finalize the Agreement)

Ask a closing question such as:

- *Are you ready to move forward at this time?*
- *Is there any reason you wouldn't want to or couldn't move forward?*
- *Would you be comfortable signing the contract today?*

If Ready   If Not Ready

Step 2: Query to Understand Their Position or Objection

Ask a clarifying question such as:

- *Is there any particular reason that you are not ready?*
- *What is it that is holding you back?*
- *Do you have any other concerns?*

Step 3: Confirm Their Position or Objection

Use a trial close to make sure you have found the real issue:

- *If we were to take care of that (those) issue(s), then would you be ready to move forward today?*

Flush out every possible objection by asking:

- *Is there any other reason you couldn't move forward?*

Step 4: Prepare Your Counteroffer, Trade-Off, or Resolution

You don't have to agree to everything your customer asks for. Take your time and prepare a counteroffer that gives them a portion of what they want in exchange for something that you want. Trade profit for profit. You may have to come up with a work-around to some condition of the sale or a way to resolve some particular issue they have. You might even need to further educate your customer or reposition your solution.

Step 5: Propose Your Counteroffer, Trade-Off, or Resolution

When ready, propose your resolution as a hypothetical question:

- *What if I couldn't offer the 10 percent discount you asked for but could agree to a 6 percent discount? Would you be willing to sign the contract today?*

Step 6: Move Forward with the Next Step (Finalize the Agreement)

Available at: **SalesExcellence.com**

Figure 9.1 The Results-Based Negotiation Process

sales cycle. It is made up of six steps. Let's walk though the process and talk in detail about what is involved in each of these steps.

Step 1: Ask Your Client to Take the Next Step (Finalize the Agreement)

The first step in the results-based negotiation process is asking your prospective client to take the next reasonable step in their buying process. This requires asking a closing question, such as:

- Are you ready to move forward at this time?
- Is there any reason you wouldn't want to or couldn't move forward?
- Would you be comfortable signing the contract today?
- Is there anything else you need at this point, or are you ready to _____ (i.e., take the next step)?

It can be helpful to recognize that we ask closing questions all the time, not just when it comes time to finalize our agreement or sign our contract. If you perceive closing the sale as just another step toward helping your customer reach point C, then asking, "Are you ready to place the order?" becomes less unsettling for both you and your customer.

A closing question helps you accomplish two important things: (1) asking your customer to make a commitment and take the next step, and (2) flushing out any objections or obstacles that would keep them from making that commitment. Asking a closing question also helps you determine if the person you are dealing with has the authority to make the commitment to move forward. In some cases, your customer will be ready to take the next step. If they're ready, you can skip to step 6 and move forward. But, if they're not ready, you'll need to find out why they're not.

Step 2: Query to Understand Their Position or Objection

If your customer is *not* ready to book the next appointment, agree to a trial of your product, issue a purchase order, or sign your contract, you need to ask them why. The reason they give you for not moving forward could be an objection. In that case, you can try to help them move past it. Their reason could also be a condition or an excuse. Let's explore the differences between a condition, an objection, and an excuse as well as how to handle all three.

A *condition* is a fact-based reason why your client can't take the next step, such as:

- The company's goals or objectives have changed, so the project that your solution is a part of has been abandoned.
- Finance has put a freeze on all capital expenditures until a merger or acquisition is completed.
- The final approver or contract signer is on vacation.
- The person who will oversee the project (project owner) just quit, and everything is on hold until a replacement is hired.

Not every condition is a complete show-stopper. Part of our job is to help our client figure out a possible work-around for a condition that is holding up their buying process. However, conditions that can't be worked around can stall or even destroy your opportunity. It's important to remain aware of the changing conditions within your prospective client's business as part of your ongoing qualification process.

Objections are different from conditions. An *objection* typically stems from how your customer feels or how they perceive the world, such as:

- Your system is too complicated for our needs.
- We know we need it, but we want to wait until next year.
- Your price is too high.

Objections can often be overcome by helping our customer see things differently. We could propose a trial of our system to prove that it is *not* too complicated. Perhaps we could put together a business case that makes the return on investment in our solution attractive enough to be acted on *this* year. Or maybe, with a little more education and positioning, we could help our customer realize that the overall value of our company, our people, and our solution is *far greater* than what our competitor offers even if they have a lower purchase price.

Often, the first reason they give you for not moving forward is actually an excuse. This is the reason they give you that sounds good on the surface, but isn't the real objection. Examples might include, "We are just too busy right now," or, "We don't have the money in our budget." It can be very difficult to tell the difference between an objection and an excuse. The only way you'll really know is by working through the rest of the results-based negotiation process that follows.

Before you can overcome an objection or come up with a workable solution for moving forward, you have to understand where your customer is coming from. If they have an objection, you'll need to understand what it is and why it's a problem.

One common objection you will hear—especially when you reach the point in the sales cycle where your customer is considering placing an order or signing a contract—is that they don't want to pay the price you have proposed. If your customer asks you for a reduction in price or requests some other kind of concession, make sure you ask them why.

The reason they give you will help you determine if the request represents a condition, an objection, or an excuse. It may also give you some idea of how to deal with the request. It is critical that you get to the real objection by drilling for the root cause of the reason they are not ready to move forward. Regardless of what they tell you, always ask, "Is there anything else?" Until you understand the real problem, you can't put together a plan for how to resolve it and move past it.

Step 3: Confirm Their Position or Objection

If you've questioned your customer—and you feel you have identified their objection to moving forward—always confirm that you fully understand the issue or what they are asking for. One excellent technique for confirming your customer's objection is using what is referred to as a trial close. Essentially, this is a way to find out if they are, in fact, interested in finding a resolution or reaching an agreement.

Confirming your prospect's objection and issuing a trial close sounds like this:

> *"John, it sounds like what's holding you back is _____. Is that right?"*
> *"Yes. That's it."*
> *"What if we were to come up with a way to eliminate this as a concern? Would you be ready to move forward right now?"*

What you're asking here is whether your customer's objection *can* be overcome or if it's possible to reach an agreement. Your customer's response should reveal whether or not you are dealing with the real issue. If their answer is, "Yes. I would be ready to move forward right now," then you can continue working through the negotiation process and work toward some kind of agreement. But other times their response will be, "No. I have another concern, too."

Repeat this process as many times as necessary to flush out every possible objection. If every trial close you attempt is met with yet another reason they can't move forward, they are probably just trying to sell you an excuse to avoid telling you their real objection to moving forward.

Sometimes your customer doesn't want to resolve all their issues or concerns. Sometimes they just don't want to move forward period. By using this approach, you should be able to ascertain whether they actually have an interest in working things out.

Step 4: Prepare Your Counteroffer, Trade-Off, or Resolution

Once you understand your customer's objection or their request for a concession, you can begin to think about whether or not you want to agree to all or part of what they have requested. The first major point to remember is that you don't have to agree to everything they ask for. Never immediately agree to any concession your customer asks for *in its entirety*. Instead, make a counteroffer that gives them *a portion* of what they want. Ultimately, you might decide you have to give them all of what they ask for in order to close the deal, but don't start there.

The second major point is that you should never give something for nothing. If you believe that your prices and other contract terms are fair, then lowering your price or altering the terms and conditions would unfairly tip the scale in your customer's favor. To rebalance the equation, it is only reasonable that you should ask for something in return.

Most salespeople know they should never give something for nothing. However, many of them don't know exactly what to ask for or how to ask for it. The key is to figure out what you would want in return for whatever your customer asks you for and be ready when they make their request.

Reducing your selling price or granting any other form of concession represents a transfer of profit from your company to your client's company. Any discount you subtract from your list price reduces your profitability and increases theirs. When you provide free shipping, free telephone support, or no-interest financing, those things aren't actually *free*. Your company has to pay for them out of whatever profit you earn. If at some point you must concede something, don't just hand over your profit without asking for something in return. Instead, trade profit for profit.

Before you enter any pricing or contract negotiations, take the time to identify what kind of objections your customer is likely to raise or what concessions they might request. These things represent profit to your client's company. Also, give some thought to what would represent profit to you and your company.

Profit for you might be a larger order or the commitment to place future orders. You might also want a longer-term service contract, introductions to buyers in other departments or divisions, or their agreement to provide testimonials and act as a reference account. Think about what you can request in exchange for whatever concessions they request from you.

To help you plan what you want to ask for, you can use what I call a trading profit for profit worksheet. Figure 9.2 shows a completed worksheet for a company that sells their products through retail stores.

If you sell enterprise software applications, your worksheet will look quite different and might include profit for your customer such as free user training, discounted software maintenance, or discounted implementation services. Profit for you might be asking your customer to buy additional user licenses that will be rolled out at a later date, additional software modules, or an introduction to the executives of their parent company. Taking the time to complete a worksheet like

Trading Profit for Profit Worksheet

Profit for Our Customer	Profit for Us
1. Lower Buying Price	1. Larger Order Commitments
2. Higher Back-End Rebates	2. Contract Extension
3. Higher Catalog Page Rates	3. Greater Wallet-Share in Category
4. Slotting Fees	4. New or Additional Categories
5. Extended Payment Terms	5. Better or More Catalog Placements
6. Goods on Consignment	6. Better or More Shelf Positions
7. Co-Op Advertising	7. Co-Op Advertising
8. Consumer and Market Research	8. Access to Executive Management
9. Category Management Assistance	9. References and/or Testimonials
10. Defective Allowances	10. Referrals (internal or external)
11. New Store Allowances	11. Bulk Deliveries
12. Return Privileges	12. Higher Buying Price

Available at: **SalesExcellence.com**

Figure 9.2 Trading Profit for Profit Worksheet

this before every significant negotiation will greatly improve your effectiveness in trading profit for profit and thus maximize your sales results.

Step 5: Propose Your Counteroffer, Trade-off, or Resolution

After you have decided what you want to ask for as a trade, propose your idea to your customer as a hypothetical resolution. Throughout this book we have talked about the power of using hypothetical questions and scenarios in a variety of sales situations. Nowhere is this approach more valuable than in negotiations.

Using a hypothetical resolution enables you to explore the possibilities with your customer without either party committing to anything. It allows you to draw a line in the sand and explore how your client feels about it. Then you and your client can rearrange and reshape the resolution until you are both happy with it before you ask them to move forward.

Here are a few examples of how you can use the hypothetical resolution:

- Suppose I was able to get approval for the discount you have asked for. Would you be willing to increase your monthly order commitment?
- Let's assume that we could alter our return policy as you have requested. Could you provide me with an introduction and a recommendation to the buyer at your Tennessee plant?
- If I could get you the pricing you want on our line of desktop accessories, would you be willing to carry our line of cell phone accessories in your stores as well?

Figure 9.3 on page 205 shows a number of different ways to set up the hypothetical and propose your resolution.

Notice the three examples near the bottom of the figure. If your customer requests something you can't or don't want to give, you can respond with, "What if I can't do that?" or, "Suppose that wasn't possible?" The hypothetical allows you to explore the consequences of saying no without actually saying it.

When you use one of these examples and combine the idea of a counteroffer *and* the hypothetical resolution, your proposal might sound like this:

- What if I am not able to waive the training fees as you've requested but am willing to provide free installation? Would you be willing to sign the contract today?

- Suppose I couldn't get approval for the 30 percent discount you asked for, but could offer you a 20 percent discount. Could you agree to making us your sole source for this product?

However you choose to use it, the hypothetical resolution gives you tremendous power and control in negotiations. It allows you to slow things down and think about what you are agreeing to before you make any commitments. Using the hypothetical resolution is probably the most powerful skill you can master in your quest to become a more effective negotiator.

Step 6: Move Forward with the Next Step (Finalize the Agreement)

When both you and your customer are comfortable with the plan to move forward, you can take the next step together. This assumes that your customer really does want to come up with a workable resolution or finalize the agreement. If your customer doesn't want to move forward, and they won't tell you why, you might have to engage with someone different within the account. If nothing you propose seems agreeable to your customer, it could be that the person you're dealing with doesn't have the authority to finalize an agreement or place an order.

When an opportunity bogs down in negotiations, it is usually a sign that the opportunity is not as highly qualified as you might think. You might need to review both why your customer would buy and how they could buy if they wanted to. Go back to the opportunity scorecard (from Chapter Five) and evaluate the opportunity again. If the opportunity is well qualified, you can almost always come up with some kind of plan to move forward together.

Hypothetical Resolutions in Negotiation

Set Up the Hypothetical	**Propose Your Resolution**
If I were to agree to . . .	Would you be ready to . . . ?
If I could get approval for . . .	Would you be able to . . . ?
What if I was willing to agree to . . .	Would you be willing to . . . ?
Suppose I was able to . . .	Would you be in a position to . . . ?
Imagine that I said "yes" to . . .	Would it be possible to . . . ?
Assume, for a minute, that I could . . .	Would there be any way you could . . . ?
If it were possible for me to . . .	Could you arrange . . . ?
Let's suppose I was able to . . .	Could you get approval to . . . ?
Let's imagine that I could . . .	Could we work together to . . . ?
Let's assume that I agreed to . . .	Could we come up with a way to . . . ?

or:

What if I couldn't . . . ?	Would you be open to . . . ?
Suppose I wasn't able to agree to . . . ?	Could we come up with a way to . . . ?
Let's imagine it was not possible to . . . ?	What would you say to the idea of . . . ?

Available at: **Sales Excellence.com**

Figure 9.3 Hypothetical Resolutions in Negotiation

Reducing Price Erosion and Maximizing Profitability

One of the primary objectives of the results-based selling method is to reduce price erosion in order to increase your average deal size and maximize profitability. Using the results-based negotiation process will help you manage the negotiation process, but there are several other principles that are critical to maximizing your results.

Get on Offense and Stay on Offense

Once you have submitted your proposal—and your customer indicates they are interested in moving forward—this is not the time to quit selling and prepare to take a beating at the negotiation table. In fact, the best thing you can do is show up on the day you plan to finalize the agreement with an alternate proposal that is larger in scope or longer in duration than the proposal you've already submitted.

Explain to your customer that you came up with a way for them to save an additional 8 percent if they were willing to license the software they will need for phases one and two of their project all at the same time. Show your retail chain buyer your new idea to help them increase their profitability by handling three different categories of your product in their stores instead of only two.

You will be amazed at how effective this technique can be if you are willing to try it. This approach will completely change the dynamic of your negotiations. If your new proposal really does offer greater value to your customer, they might just take you up on it. I have successfully used this technique countless times. If they are not interested in your new ideas, you haven't lost anything. When you settle back to your original proposal, you will have already made your first concession.

Always stay proactive, even as you enter the final negotiation stage of an opportunity. The worst thing you can do is shut down, hold your breath, and brace yourself for whatever your customer demands while hoping that there is still a little profit left after they get through working you over. Get on offense and stay on offense as much as you can.

Learn to Score on Defense

There will be times when your customer requests or even demands certain concessions. This isn't always a negative. It could actually be an opportunity! As we talked about earlier, when they ask you for something they want, that gives you license to ask for something you want. But instead of proposing what might be perceived as an even trade, ask for something much greater than what they ask you for.

Throughout this book we talk about the three ways to maximize sales revenue: increasing deal size, accelerating sales velocity, and improving sales predictability. When your customer asks you for a concession, think about how you can propose a trade that will have a positive impact on one or more of these three measures. Make your counteroffer, and then ask for something else too!

If your customer asks you to reduce your price by 10 percent, you could counter by offering to reduce the price per unit by 6 percent if they agree to order 25 units instead of 20 (i.e., grow the deal size). If they want you to provide free training to *all* the people who will use your system, you could counter by offering to train *two* people for free, but only if they are willing to place next month's order this month (i.e., accelerate the sale). If they ask you to extend their payment terms from 30 to 60 days, you could counter by offering to extend the terms to 45 days if they will sign a one-year contract ensuring a minimum monthly order commitment (i.e., improve sales predictability).

Anytime your customer asks you for something, try to come up with a trade that makes the transaction and the relationship even more valuable to you than it was before. Always look for opportunities to score, even when you are playing defense.

Negotiate Only One Time

Have you ever been asked to provide a quote with your "best price," so your client can work it into their budget, only to have them call you back when it comes time to buy and ask for an ever bigger discount?

When you negotiate more than once, you end up giving away more profit each time. Your customers know this, and many of them will use it as a strategy to extort profit from you.

Do everything you possibly can to negotiate only one time. Avoid quoting your "best price" for budgetary purposes. Help your customer understand that your pricing is fair, your profit margins are not extreme, and that you simply can't drop the price over and over. Convince them that you can't quote your best price unless they are ready to place the order *right now!*

Negotiate Only with the Person Who Can Buy

One way that buyers try to negotiate more than once is to make you negotiate with multiple people. Clem tells you to "give us your best price" before he submits the purchase request. Then the COO (the investment owner) asks you to provide free training as part of the deal. Once the request gets to procurement, the purchasing agent tells you, "Your direct competitor just quoted the same product for 20 percent less." Sometimes they'll tell you this even if it isn't true.

Be careful that you don't give away all your profit before you even get to the person who can place the order. Explain to Clem and the COO that you can consider their request for a concession only when they are ready to buy because your management simply won't approve any discounts or freebies until the order is imminent.

Your customer might try to scare you by saying, "Your competitor is willing to accept all our requests." Don't cave in to this. If they are trying to negotiate with you, you are probably their vendor of choice. Help them understand that you are not necessarily saying no, but that you can't say yes to anything until you are negotiating with the person who can actually sign the contract or issue the purchase order.

Negotiate Only When Your Customer Can Buy

Sometimes your customer wants to negotiate long before they are ready to commit to doing business with you. This should be avoided if at all possible. If you don't understand their buying process and all the approvers and influencers involved, you could end up negotiating with the *hope* that they will place the order right away. But if there are five more steps in their buying process, such as getting final approval from Corporate or obtaining funding from Finance, maybe they can't buy for another week—or even a month!

A lot can change during that time. The project could be postponed or scrapped altogether. There might be personnel changes that disrupt the buying process. Another vendor could circle back with a low-ball quote. When they eventually get to the point where they *can* buy, you might find yourself having to renegotiate the deal and offer even more incentives.

Negotiate Everything at the Same Time

Another technique that buyers use is negotiating with you to get a rock-bottom price and then coming back two days later to ask for extended payment terms. If they get their way with that, they might come back even later to negotiate other aspects of the deal such as minimum order requirements or the right to return merchandise they don't sell.

We should try to negotiate everything that is negotiable all at the same time. If your customer says, "We need you to reduce the purchase price by 10 percent," tell them, "I'm not sure that's possible. But before we could even consider that, I would need to know that you are satisfied with all the other terms and conditions of the agreement."

If they have any other issues or concerns, get them all on the table at the same time. Then you can propose a resolution that addresses all of them. Don't leave yourself exposed to requests for other kinds of concessions *after* you have negotiated the price.

Don't Negotiate with Yourself

Sometimes, in an effort to maximize their own profits, your customer will try to squeeze more profit out of you by saying something like, "You need to sharpen your pencil." Or, "You'll have to do better than that." Don't just start dropping your price with the hope that they will tell you when it's low enough. Respond to any request for a concession by asking, "Why do you say that, Bob?"

Assuming they have a valid reason for requesting it, make them quantify the concession by asking, "What did you have in mind?" If they don't like the pricing or terms you have proposed, then they need to tell you what they don't like about them. You could ask, "What part of this proposal are you not comfortable with?" Followed by, "Is there anything else?"

Avoid asking, "Where do we need to be?" That suggests that you have virtually unlimited flexibility and that they can set your price for you. The idea is to get *them* to drive a stake in the ground where *they* would like to be. Then you can see how far apart you really are and come up with a resolution that is acceptable to both parties.

Never Match Price

We've all probably had a customer ask us to reduce our purchase price to match that of some other vendor. They might say, "Your competitor quoted the same thing at half the price." That may not be true. It could easily be a ploy to see how far you are willing to go to win the deal.

If you become convinced that your customer really does have an alternative source who offers a lower price that they ask you to match, work through the following five questions to see if you can command a premium:

1. If They Were Both the Same Price, Which One Would You Rather Have? This question will help you determine whether your prospective client really wants to do business with you or is just using you as leverage to drive down some other vendor's price. Your customer may say they'd rather do business with the other vendor. In that case, you actually lost the deal long ago. If they tell you, "I'd rather do business with you!" then ask them to explain …

2. Why? There has to be some reason why they would prefer to buy from you. See if they will tell you what it is about your company, your people, or your solution that they consider to be better. Regardless of what they point out, ask if there are any other reasons why they would rather work with you. Write down each reason on a white board or a piece of paper. Once you have a list of why they think you offer a better package, ask them …

3. Isn't That Worth Anything? Are Those Things Valueless to You? Ask them to explain how the advantages they pointed out will enable them to complete their project faster, earn a greater ROI, minimize their risks, and so on. Get them to sell you on why those things matter. If they are able to appreciate any added value, ask …

4. How Much Are Those Differences Worth? See if they can quantify the added value that you bring to the table. You may need to help them estimate what that would be worth to them in dollars and cents. Keep your discussion centered on value to them as opposed to who has the lowest price. If you and your customer can translate the added value into a dollar figure, then ask …

5. So Are You Saying That If Our Price Were _____ More, We Could Do Business? Most of my clients find that they can command a 10 to 20 percent premium by using this technique, and some have reported even more than that. This all depends, of course, on how well you have positioned yourself before the negotiation started.

*   *   *

Some percentage of buyers will still ask you to match the lowest bid, and you can choose whether you want to match it or walk away. At least you will be validating whatever price you do charge, which makes your buyer feel they received fair value for their money.

Be Willing to Walk Away

There are opportunities that aren't worth winning if you have to give away all your profit—or even go in the hole—in order to close the deal. Only you and your company's management can decide how far you are willing to go to get the business, but in some cases, you might be better off to simply walk away. Unless walking away is one of your options, you might begin to feel desperate and obligated to accept whatever terms and conditions your customer dictates.

As I mention in Chapter Three, a salesperson will almost never walk away from an opportunity unless they have another one to walk toward. Therefore, one of the things that determines your effectiveness in negotiations is the health of your opportunity portfolio. You have to know that you can survive without closing any one particular deal before you can negotiate with confidence.

At some point, you will have to decide where your "line" is. What is the most you are willing to give up to close the opportunity? You should also try to determine where your customer's line is. What is the most they are willing to pay? Don't be afraid to talk about what they might do if you can't grant all their requests. In fact, it's vital that you know what alternatives they have in mind.

One way to find your customer's line is to respond to their request for a concession by saying, "That's more than I can do." Then, keep your mouth closed. Wait for them to speak. Their reaction will often tell you whether they really want to work with you or have a backup plan in case you don't meet all their demands.

Sometimes, the only way to locate their line is by drawing a line of your own. You can understand more about their options and explore the consequences of walking away by posing a hypothetical scenario, like these:

- What if our bid is not the lowest one that you receive?
- What if one of the vendors you are considering came in with a significantly lower price?
- Suppose I wasn't able to grant your request for a concession, Mr. Jamison. What would you do then?

Remember, you don't have to grant every concession your customer asks for, so you shouldn't feel that you are at their mercy. In most cases, if you use the hypothetical resolution to explore the possibilities, you can come up with a counteroffer that works for both parties. In the end, the deal has to deliver favorable results for your customer *and* for you.

* * *

Learning to apply the concepts and techniques within this chapter will make you far more effective at handling customer objections, negotiating price and contract terms, and bringing business to closure. Again, you don't have to meet every demand that your customer makes. You have an obligation to yourself and to your company to minimize price erosion and maximize your sales revenue. Learning how to maintain price integrity and profitability is a vital aspect of improving your sales results.

CHAPTER TEN

Implementing the Results-Based Selling Method

Now that you have been introduced to all the components of the results-based selling method, the question on your mind probably is, "How can I make this system work for me?" The good news is that it is already starting to work because all positive change in your sales behavior starts with changing the way you think. All you have to do now is start putting these new ideas to use.

In this chapter, we talk about how to employ the results-based approach as a five-step process to help you define and reach your sales goals and objectives. As part of this process, we walk through a 16-point checklist designed to help you integrate the various tools, templates, and worksheets presented here into your selling environment. Then, we discuss the role that sales managers and other executives play in the successful adoption of this program.

Applying the Results-Based Approach

To make the most of the material in this book, you will need to apply the results-based approach—which you use to help your customers reach their goals—to setting and reaching your own sales goals. The results-based approach to goal achievement can be summed up as a five-step process:

> **Step one:** Determine where you are now.
> **Step two:** Decide where you want to be in the future.
> **Step three:** Develop your plan of action.
> **Step four:** Execute your plan.
> **Step five:** Measure your results.

This five-step process is the foundation of the results-based selling method. It can be used in a wide variety of situations to help you define and achieve your desired sales results. As we explore step four of this process, we talk about how to execute your plan of action using a 16-point checklist to implement the results-based selling tool set. Let's walk through each of these five steps and talk about how to apply these concepts in your sales environment.

Step One: Determine Where You Are Now

By now, you probably won't be surprised to read that I recommend beginning by determining where you are now before you define what you hope to accomplish in the future. Think about how you are doing currently. How much of this year's revenue goals have you already achieved? What are your sales results to date?

You will probably be able to quickly determine your sales revenue year-to-date and the percentage of your annual quota you have attained so far this year. But I would like to ask you to also look at three more vitally important measures:

1. What is the average size of your sales transactions (i.e., deal size)?

2. How many opportunities are you closing each month or each quarter, and how long is your average sales cycle (i.e., sales velocity)?

3. Out of all the revenue you forecast to close, how much of it actually closes when you think it will (i.e., sales predictability)?

Every increase in sales revenue is a direct result of an improvement in one of these three measures. Therefore, if you want to increase revenue, begin to focus on growing the size of each opportunity, managing more opportunities at one time and closing them faster, and prioritizing your investment of time and energy on the opportunities that are most likely to close in a timely manner. If you haven't been tracking this kind of information, then you may not be able to establish a baseline just yet.

If you can, go back and look at whatever data you have. See if you can determine the average size of your transactions, the average length of your sales cycle, or the accuracy of your forecasts. If this approach is something new, you can start using the results-based selling method as you begin to gather this information. What we are trying to determine is your *current state* using measures that we can track going forward to monitor your progress toward your goals.

Step Two: Decide Where You Want to Be in the Future

To make the most of the results-based selling method, define exactly what you want to accomplish. Don't settle for an ambiguous goal such as, "I want to sell more." Goals that are vague don't motivate, and they make it difficult for you to measure your progress. Try to be as specific as you can about your *desired future state* and what you want to accomplish.

Once you know where you are now, you can set goals that are aggressive but also realistic. If you carry an annual sales quota, then one of your primary goals is already set for you. The key is to take account of where you are and what it's going to take to get to your desired destination. Then you can put together a plan to make it happen. Working hard and hoping for the best is a start, but a clearly defined objective and a plan of action to achieve it are what separate the amateur from the professional.

Your goals should be specific, measurable, and time-bound. For example, a strong goal would be to increase average deal size from $42,000 to $50,000 by the end of the fiscal year. All other things being equal, that alone would produce a 20 percent increase in your revenue results.

Other excellent goals might be to reduce the average length of sales cycles from 136 to 120 days by the end of next fiscal quarter, or to increase the accuracy of sales forecasts from 52 percent to 65 percent over the next 6 months. Having a goal to increase revenue is great! But the way you achieve that goal is by increasing deal size, velocity, and predictability.

By establishing clearly defined objectives, you will naturally start to focus your effort in the right place. Working harder and increasing activity are noble gestures, but they don't necessarily lead to an increase in sales results unless your energies are channeled toward a specific objective.

Step Three: Develop Your Plan of Action

When you know what you want to accomplish and how you will measure and track your progress, it's time to develop a plan of action to make it happen. Look at the goals you have established and ask yourself, "What do I need to do differently to get this done?" If you've read even a portion of this book, you are probably already starting to look at your world in a different way. Let your new way of thinking drive new behaviors.

To support these new ways of thinking and behaving, you may need to employ new processes, systems, or tools. The results-based selling method offers a broad array of tools designed to help you accomplish specific sales results. If you want to, you can adopt every tool presented in this book. Some organizations will choose to do that over time. But for now, you might want to select a few of these tools that represent the best opportunities to improve your sales results.

Part of your plan of action will be to integrate all or part of the results-based selling tool set into whatever processes or structure you already have in place. For this example, let us assume that your plan of action includes implementing the entire set of tools, templates, and worksheets introduced in this book.

Step Four: Execute Your Plan

Once you have identified where you are and where you want to be and have developed your plan of action, it's time to roll up your sleeves and *do it*. Commit to your plan of action and execute. The key is to stay consistent and persistent and see your plan through to completion. Now let's talk about how to execute your plan to implement the entire results-based selling tool set using a 16-point checklist.

The 16-Point Implementation Checklist

The following is a 16-point implementation checklist that will help you to employ all the tools, templates, and worksheets presented throughout this book. Some of these tools are designed to help you better manage sales opportunities, while others have been created to promote your own personal development. The implementation checklist, in Figure 10.1, shows all 16 points and the various tools, templates, and worksheets used in each.

Let's look at the 16-point checklist for implementing the system in more detail:

1. Organize Your Opportunity Portfolio. Use a list of your current sales opportunities to create an opportunity portfolio as shown in Figure 10.2. If you use a CRM or SFA system, it will probably create a report like this from your account and opportunity database.

The key elements of an opportunity portfolio (pipeline report) are:

- The name of the account and/or opportunity.
- A description of the opportunity.
- An estimate of how much revenue the opportunity represents.
- The date you expect the opportunity will come to closure.
- The probability of winning the opportunity (as a percentage).
- The weighted revenue (the estimated revenue multiplied by the probability percentage).

Using the information you already have, estimate the revenue of each opportunity as well as the date you expect the opportunity to come to closure. If you currently use a process for evaluating the probability of each opportunity, use that to determine the weighted revenue that each opportunity represents. This is where you will start from as you begin to implement the results-based selling system. As you find new sales opportunities going forward, add them to your opportunity portfolio accordingly.

16-Point Implementation Checklist

Numbers in parentheses represent corresponding tools (figures) in *Selling Results!*

1. Organize Your Opportunity Portfolio
- ☐ Opportunity Portfolio (10.2)

2. Qualify Each Opportunity with the Opportunity Scorecard
- ☐ Opportunity Review Sheet (6.6)
- ☐ Opportunity Scorecard (5.1)
- ☐ Opportunity Scorecard Guidelines 1-10 (5.6)
- ☐ Opportunity Scorecard Guidelines 11-20 (5.7)

3. Size or Resize Each Opportunity
- ☐ Using the ideas in Chapters Four and Six, identify and earn your way to the project owner, investment owner, and the final approver and size or resize each opportunity based on their input.

4. Frame Each Opportunity in Time
- ☐ Questions for Framing the Opportunity (6.2)
- ☐ Reverse-Engineering Worksheet (6.3)

5. Create a Weighted Revenue Projection to Estimate Future Revenues
- ☐ Weighted Revenue Projection (10.3)

6. Evaluate What It Will Take to Achieve Your Sales Goals
- ☐ Sales Activity Planning Sheet (1.1)

7. Make a Commitment to Consistent Business Development
- ☐ 30-Day Business Development Plan (3.7)
- ☐ Company Research Template (3.3)
- ☐ Executive Research Template (3.4)
- ☐ Outbound Business Development Process (3.2)
- ☐ Eight-Pronged Approach Worksheet (3.5)
- ☐ Business Development Worksheet (3.6)

8. Broaden Your Relationship Footprint within Each Account
- ☐ Buying Roles Exercise (4.1)
- ☐ Roles Involved in a Buying Process [sheet] (4.2)
- ☐ Buying Roles Chart (4.3)

9. Develop a Joint Plan to Move Each Opportunity Forward
- ☐ Reverse-Engineering Worksheet (6.3)
- ☐ Customer Results Plan (6.5)

10. Plan Your Meetings and Phone Calls to Maximize Results
- ☐ Opportunity Review Sheet (6.6)
- ☐ Precall Planning Sheet (6.7)

11. Further Develop Your Questioning Skills
- ☐ Questions about Why Customers Buy (5.3)
- ☐ Hypothetical Questions to Explore Point C (5.2)
- ☐ Questions about How Customers Buy (5.5)
- ☐ Hypothetical Questions about the Buying Process (6.4)

12. Increase the Effectiveness of Your Sales Presentations
- ☐ Executive Presentation Template (See Chapter Eight)
- ☐ Tying Your Capabilities to Your Client's Goals [slides] (8.1)

13. Improve Your Effectiveness in Closing and Negotiating Opportunities
- ☐ Results-Based Negotiation Process (9.1)
- ☐ Trading Profit for Profit Worksheet (9.2)
- ☐ Hypothetical Resolutions in Negotiation (9.3)

14. Develop Your Business Acumen and Your Fluency in the Language of Business
- ☐ Sample Income Statement (7.3)
- ☐ Sample Balance Sheet (7.4)
- ☐ Sample Return on Investment Projection (7.5)
- ☐ Capabilities and Results Sheet (7.6)
- ☐ Customer Results Maps (7.7 and Appendix)

15. Make Sure Your Marketing Message Supports the Results-Based Approach
- ☐ Capabilities and Results Sheet (7.6)

16. Constantly Focus on Maximizing Your Sales Results
- ☐ Sales Results Scorecard (10.5)

Available at: **SalesExcellence.com**

Figure 10.1 16-Point Implementation Checklist

Opportunity Portfolio

Date: April 11
Period: This Fiscal Year
Group: Mid-Atlantic Territory

Opportunities	Description	Estimated Revenue	Date Expected	Probability Weighting	Weighted Revenue
Apax Manufacturing	SCM Enterprise, 18 users	$165,850	04/22/XX	76%	$126,046
Delta Communications	SCM Midmarket, 8 users	$90,000	04/30/XX	61%	$54,900
Echo Pharmaceuticals	SCM Enterprise, 10 users	$148,000	05/15/XX	51%	$75,480
Tank Master, Inc.	SCM Enterprise, 24 users	$225,000	06/30/XX	74%	$166,500
Barronson Technologies	SCM Midmarket	$68,000	07/28/XX	66%	$44,880
ADG, Inc.	SCM Enterprise, 5 users	$124,250	09/24/XX	48%	$59,640
Up-Time Services, Inc.	SCM Midmarket	$68,000	09/30/XX	55%	$37,400
Appleton Manufacturing	SCM Enterprise, 22 users	$218,500	09/30/XX	24%	$52,440
Masterpiece Industries	SCM Foundation, 10 users	$82,500	10/29/XX	15%	$12,375
Total Construction, Inc.	SCM Enterprise, 12 users	$155,800	12/18/XX	33%	$51,414
DTX Proto-Tools	SCM Midmarket	$68,000	12/31/XX	27%	$18,360
Smith & Andrews, Inc.	SCM Foundation	$42,500	12/31/XX	18%	$7,650
	Total:	$1,456,400		**Weighted Total:**	$707,085

Available at: **Sales Excellence.com**

Figure 10.2 Opportunity Portfolio

2. Qualify Each Opportunity with the Opportunity Scorecard. Carefully review each opportunity in your portfolio. It is helpful to use the opportunity review sheet (Figure 6.6) to begin this process to help you determine what you know and don't know about each account. Then, use the opportunity scorecard (Figure 5.1) and the opportunity scorecard guidelines (Figures 5.6 and 5.7) to evaluate the quality of the opportunity. This exercise will prompt you to consider your customer's current state (point A), their desired future state (point C), their vision of the ideal solution (B), and the six action drivers as well as all the different aspects of their buying process.

Once you score each opportunity to determine its likelihood of coming to closure, use the total score as a percentage to calculate the probability of that opportunity. I encourage you to compare this probability percentage to the one your current forecasting system calculates—if you have one. You might choose to use this new way of gauging probability, stick with the old one, or use them in combination. One added benefit of the opportunity scorecard is that it helps you identify exactly what you need to do to improve the quality of the opportunity and make it more likely to close.

3. Size or Resize Each Opportunity. Using the concepts introduced in Chapters Four and Six, access the key players involved in your customer's buying process, size or resize each opportunity based on input from the project owner, the investment owner, and the final approver. Be careful not to estimate the size of the opportunity based on input from a low-level contact (Clem) or a selection committee. Get a feel for the scope of the project and your client's appetite for investment from the people who are responsible for earning a return on whatever capital they decide to invest.

4. Frame Each Opportunity in Time. Evaluate (or reevaluate) the expected close date for each opportunity in your portfolio using the concept of framing introduced in Chapter Six. Apply the questions for framing the opportunity (Figure 6.2) to determine:

- Urgency: When do they need to arrive at point C?
- Motive: Why do they need to arrive at point C at that time?
- Consequence: What if they don't arrive at point C at that time?

Once you understand the time frame of when your customer needs to arrive at point C, then you can work backward to reverse-engineer their buying and utilization processes using the reverse-engineering worksheet (Figure 6.3). This will give you a very reliable estimate of when this customer will buy that is based on their urgency to achieve their desired business results, not our urgency to sell something.

5. Create a Weighted Revenue Projection to Estimate Future Revenues. Now that you have sized and framed the deals in your opportunity portfolio, you can turn it into a weighted revenue projection as shown in Figure 10.3. This is a visual representation of the weighted revenue in your opportunity portfolio. A report like this helps to reveal any weaknesses in your portfolio while you still have time to do something about it.

This sample report shows your current projected revenue for each month compared to your monthly goals for the year. Projecting future sales revenue is a very important part of sales planning. If your average sales cycle is 120 days, for example, then *next* quarter's sales results are already being shaped by the quantity and the quality of the opportunities in *this* quarter's opportunity portfolio (pipeline). Therefore, your ability to influence next quarter's revenue results lies in the actions you take *today!*

6. Evaluate What It Will Take to Achieve Your Sales Goals. Once you have a good understanding of what's in your current opportunity portfolio, you can begin to plan what else is going to be required to reach your sales goals. Use the sales activity planning sheet (Figure 1.1) to estimate how many more opportunities you will need to identify, qualify, and engage. This can then be translated into monthly and weekly business development activity goals that will ensure you achieve your revenue objective.

7. Make a Commitment to Consistent Business Development. Reaching your revenue goals will require consistent and persistent business development effort. Create a 30-day business development plan (Figure 3.7) employing the principles and tools introduced in Chapter Three.

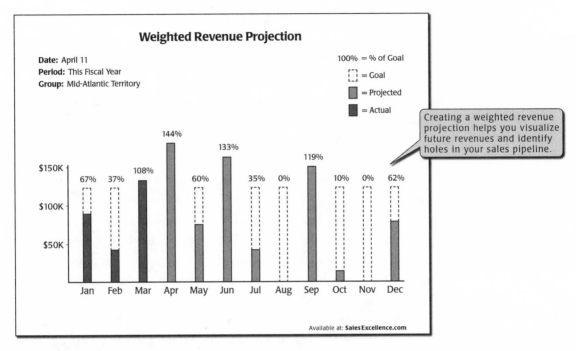

Figure 10.3 Weighted Revenue Projection

Begin using the outbound business development process (Figure 3.2) or, if necessary, create your own process that is perfectly suited to your sales environment.

Use the company research template (Figure 3.3) and the executive research template (Figure 3.4) to help you gather the information you need before you reach out to your prospective client. Then, use the eight-pronged approach worksheet (Figure 3.5) and the business development worksheet (Figure 3.6) to help you manage the process and track your results.

8. Broaden Your Relationship Footprint within Each Account. Identify who you currently know within each account using the buying roles exercise (Figure 4.1). Then, review the list of roles involved in a buying process (Figure 4.2) to help you decide who else you need to meet going forward. Your objective should be to meet as many of the people who will play a role in your customer's buying process as you can. Try to meet at least one new person every time you visit each client. Create and maintain a current buying roles chart (Figure 4.3) for each opportunity that will change and grow as you build your relationship footprint within the account.

9. Develop a Joint Plan to Move Each Opportunity Forward. Assuming a sales opportunity has been properly framed (i.e., you've established a time frame for when your customer needs to reach point C), you can work backward to reverse-engineer their buying process and utilization process using the reverse-engineering worksheet (Figure 6.3) as described under point 4. Then turn that timeline into a customer results plan (Figure 6.5).

Your customer results plan is a project plan complete with dates for each event as well as the people who should be involved from both your company and your client's company. Ideally, your customer will buy in to your plan and help manage the process with you. Regardless of whether they do or not, using the plan to manage your own activity is well worth the effort. This will help you better allocate your own sales resources and enable you to manage more opportunities at a time.

10. Plan Your Meetings and Phone Calls to Maximize Results. One of the primary goals of the results-based selling method is to help sales people accomplish more during every sales meeting or phone call. First, use the opportunity review sheet (Figure 6.6) to determine what you know about an opportunity based on whatever interactions you have already had with a client. Then, use the precall planning sheet (Figure 6.7) to plan what you need to say or do at your next meeting or during your next phone call. To maximize sales velocity, every interaction with your customer should be used as a chance to move the sales opportunity forward and help the customer take one or more steps in their buying process.

11. *Further Develop Your Questioning Skills.* Your expertise in asking the right questions has a huge impact on your ability to properly qualify opportunities and influence how and why your customers buy. Throughout this book, there have been a number of tools devoted to the development of questioning skills. There are questions about why customers buy (Figure 5.3) as well as questions about how customers buy (Figure 5.5) presented in Chapter Five to aid you in the use of the opportunity scorecard.

There are also examples of how to use the powerful hypothetical question structure both to better understand your customer's point C (Figure 5.2) and to better understand their buying process (Figure 6.4). Frequent review of these examples will help you weave more of these kinds of questions into conversations with your customers and thus manage sales opportunities more effectively.

12. *Increase the Effectiveness of Your Sales Presentations.* Delivering a presentation that moves your opportunity forward is a vital skill for every sales professional. Review Chapter Eight before you begin preparing for your next group presentation. Make sure you know why you are presenting, who you are presenting to, and what you want them to think differently or do differently after you are finished. Consider using all or part of the executive presentation template (from Chapter Eight) as you craft and deliver your next executive-level presentation—especially the two slides that show how the capabilities of your solutions tie to the achievement of your client's goals (Figure 8.1).

13. *Improve Your Effectiveness in Closing and Negotiating Opportunities.* One of the most important skills of the sales profession is negotiating and bringing opportunities to closure. In Chapter Nine

I introduce a number of tools and techniques designed to help sales-people become more effective in negotiations. Reviewing and practic-ing the techniques of the results-based negotiation process (Figure 9.1), as well as using the trading profit for profit worksheet (Figure 9.2) and the hypothetical resolutions in negotiation (Figure 9.3) will help you to reduce price erosion and increase profitability by giving away less at the negotiation table.

14. Develop Your Business Acumen and Your Fluency in the Language of Business. To become more effective selling to executives, we have to learn to think like executives and communicate using the terms of business and finance. Use the tools introduced in Chapter Seven such as the sample income statement (Figure 7.3), the sample balance sheet (Figure 7.4), and the sample return on investment projection (Figure 7.5) to help you better understand how companies measure their financial success and make investment decisions.

Also, work to improve your ability to translate the functional ca-pabilities of your solutions into business results for your customers by using the capabilities and results sheet (Figure 7.6) and the customer results map (Figure 7.7). Both of these tools will help you develop expertise and confidence in selling financial results to executives.

15. Make Sure Your Marketing Message Supports the Results-Based Approach. Making the most of the results-based selling method re-quires aligning marketing with sales by creating sales tools and mar-keting collateral that are consistent with the results-based approach. If your marketing message is built around "who we are and what we do," it reinforces the broadcast approach to selling.

If your internal product training is focused on features and func-tions and how your products are superior to those of your competition, then it's only natural for salespeople to focus on that when they get in front of a prospective customer. Making the transition from selling products to selling results requires cooperation between your sales and marketing departments to change the very language in which you communicate to customers. Tools like the capabilities and results sheet (Figure 7.6) can be very useful in creating marketing materials that focus on your customer's desired outcomes and results as well as what impact your solutions can have on the various departments within your customer's organization.

16. Constantly Focus on Maximizing Your Sales Results. One of the most important truths of human behavior is, "Where performance is measured, performance improves." That's why I am such a strong proponent of measuring and managing your sales activity and results. Focusing on increasing deal size, maximizing sales velocity, and improving sales predictability leads to revenue growth—not just once in a while, but every time.

Whenever you think about any particular opportunity, continually ask yourself:

- How could I make this opportunity a little bit bigger?
- How could I close this opportunity a little bit sooner?
- How can I be a little bit more certain that this opportunity will close when I think it will?

These questions will get your creative mind involved in coming up with new ideas and help you recognize opportunities to increase your sales results when you see them. In the next section, I introduce what I call the sales results scorecard (Figure 10.5), which can help you stay focused on your goals and track your progress as you work to maximize your results.

Step Five: Measure Your Results

As you execute your plan, you will need to periodically evaluate your results. After the first 30 days, look again at your opportunity portfolio and see how much more weighted revenue you are tracking than you were a month before. Also look at your average deal size to see if there are any improvements. It usually takes longer than 30 days to see changes in the length of your sales cycles and in forecast accuracy. But you should start to see measurable results in 60 to 90 days.

Look to see what kind of results you've produced with your business development activity. If you haven't added many new opportunities to your portfolio, at least evaluate your success in terms of your conversion rates for approaches, phone conversations, and introductory meetings. It often takes more than 30 days to see marked improvements in conversion rates, but you should be able to tell if what you are doing is working.

The number of different metrics you choose to measure is up to you. As I have mentioned before, looking at deal size, length of sales cycles, and forecast accuracy is a great place to start. As you become more comfortable with this system, you can begin to track other measures that might help you further maximize your results.

When you are ready, you can begin looking at the causes of deal size, velocity, and predictability as shown in Figure 10.4. By tracking a measure like dollars at list price, you will start thinking about how to grow the size of each transaction. You'll start thinking about the various add-ons that you could include in your proposal to form a more complete solution for your customer. You'll start talking to your client about upgrading to the larger capacity or the deluxe model. Focusing on the causes of increased deal size helps you figure out what you can do to increase the size of each opportunity.

Measuring Your Success with the Sales Results Scorecard

To make the most of this concept, sales organizations or individuals can begin tracking their results with what I call a sales results scorecard, such as the one shown in Figure 10.5. This is simply a

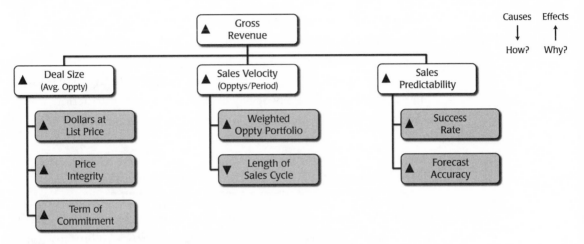

Figure 10.4 The Causes of Deal Size, Velocity and Predictability

report displaying the actual results for all the measures that were shown in the previous model (Figure 10.4).

This scorecard reports gross revenue at the top. It shows the three primary measures of deal size, sales velocity, and sales predictability. It also reports the latest figures for several other contributing factors arranged hierarchically as in Figure 10.4. It shows the unit of measure for each metric, the results for last period (last fiscal quarter in this example), the results for the current period (quarter), and the percentage of improvement for each. Note that an improvement in dollars at list price is an increase, while an improvement in the length of your average sales cycle is a decrease.

By using this kind of scorecard, you can track your progress over time. You can see how changing the way you sell and focusing on improving your results on one or more of these metrics has a direct impact on gross revenue. The value of creating a scorecard is in breaking down the big goal of increasing revenue into smaller goals so you can better focus your efforts for the greatest possible impact.

The greatest benefit of using a sales results scorecard comes not just in measuring your performance after the fact, but in influencing your thinking and behavior in the present and the future. Your scorecard becomes much more than just a stagnant measurement device. It becomes a forward-looking tool that prompts salespeople and their managers to ask, "What can be done with each active sales opportunity to maximize our sales results?" When properly developed and put into action, it will drive major changes in thinking and major improvements in results.

The Manager's Role in Implementation

If you are a manager, an executive, or a business owner and you want your sales team to make the transition from selling products to selling results, you will have to lead them in that direction. This might require a change not only in behavior but also in the very language you use to communicate with your team. You will need to show them by example how you want them to think differently and what you want them to do differently.

Management vs. Leadership

There is a marked difference between managing a sales team and leading a sales team. Managing is telling people what to do and monitoring their performance. Leadership, on the other hand, involves showing people what to do by your own actions. As a sales manager or executive, you will need the skills of both a manager and a leader to help your team accomplish their objectives. You may also need to play the role of a coach to help your people learn how to duplicate the new behavior you are modeling.

The transition from salesperson to sales manager can be difficult for some. The skills and temperament that make a great salesperson are not always the same as those that make a great sales manager. If

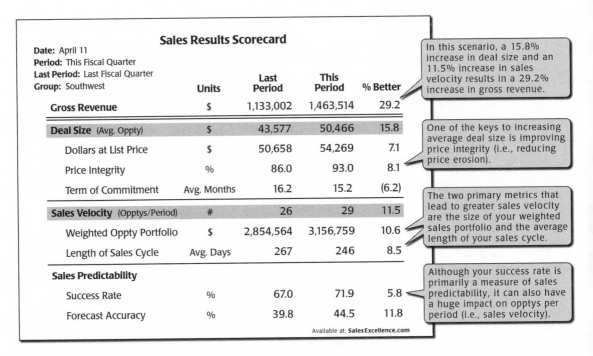

Figure 10.5 The Sales Results Scorecard

you oversee a team of six sales reps, you'll probably find that you are dealing with several different personality types and behavior styles. It's your job to lead the team in a common direction and to help each of your people reach their full potential.

The most important difference between managers and leaders is how their people respond to them. Most salespeople avoid managers as much as possible. But salespeople are naturally drawn to a leader. A manager pushes. A leader pulls. A manager focuses on minimums. A leader focuses on maximums. A leader inspires their team by their enthusiasm, optimism, and commitment to make things happen.

The key for you, as a leader, is to establish direction and goals for the team and to follow a replicable method to manage each account and opportunity. Sales strategies will vary, but your philosophy of selling needs to be steady and predictable. If you are not consistent in how you evaluate and qualify opportunities or what you do to bring opportunities to closure, your salespeople will quickly get confused and begin to replicate your inconsistency.

Modeling the Right Attitudes and Behavior

As a sales leader, you have to model the attitudes and behavior you want your team to follow. If you want your people to be results-oriented and client-focused, then don't ride along to their client meetings and start broadcasting. If you want your people to frame the opportunity and reverse-engineer the customer's buying process to establish the expected close date, then don't push them to close the deal before it is ready to be closed.

Your sales people will do what you do, not what you say. If you abandon your sales philosophy at the end of every fiscal quarter, don't be surprised when your salespeople abandon your philosophy altogether. As a general rule of thumb, your team will do about half as much of what you do right and twice as much of what you do wrong.

One of the most important things you can bring to your role is a system that you adhere to and consistently instill and impart to your team. Your team needs a common language to evaluate opportunities as well as to strategize and plan sales activity. It doesn't necessarily have to be 100 percent results-based selling, but it needs to be clear, cohesive, and consistent.

If you believe that the concepts and approaches that you have read here could help your team improve their sales results, then select some portion of the results-based selling tool set and start using it. Then help your team learn how to use it too.

Getting Your People to Use the Results-Based Selling Tools

As you've read through this book, you may have identified several techniques or tools that you would like your sales people to start using. The trick is to help your salespeople decide that they *want* to use them. Don't waste your time telling people to use the tools. In fact, the more you tell them to use the tools, the more resistance you'll get. Instead, follow these three important guidelines:

1. Focus on the Right Goals and Objectives. The goal is not to get people to fill out forms. The goal is to increase revenue. Break down your revenue goals into the smaller goals of increasing deal size, maximizing sales velocity, and improving sales predictability. Then break down each of those into yet smaller goals that your people can get their arms around. When you establish challenging but attainable goals—and sell your team on why those goals are important—your people will be much more open to using tools that can help them achieve those goals.

2. Show Them How the Tools Can Help Them Achieve Their Goals and Objectives. Once you have established the right goals, your people will have the motive they need to start using the results-based selling tools, but they may not know how to use them. If you want to increase sales velocity, for example, you might begin by focusing on increasing the number of opportunities in the sales pipeline. Sit down with each of your salespeople and, using the sales activity planning sheet (Figure 1.1) and the 30-day business development plan (Figure 3.7), help them establish their business development goals for the next 30 days.

You might also need to sit down and show them how the business development worksheet (Figure 3.6) or the eight-pronged approach worksheet (Figure 3.5) can help them be more consistent in their prospecting activities and substantially shorten the length of their business development cycle. At the end of the month, review their results and help them adjust their activity goals to ensure that they achieve their desired sales results.

3. Don't Confuse Them. Once you set the goals and the agenda for the team—and you establish the process and the plan for each salesperson to achieve their goals—don't knock them off track by abandoning your philosophy the last two weeks of every quarter. When your people believe that you have changed course, they tend to change with you. If you change your plan too often, they'll soon conclude that they can't keep up. Then they'll give up trying to follow any system and start living from lead to lead. Be careful not to sabotage your salespeople's success and in the process ultimately sabotage your own.

Using the Results-Based Selling Tools Yourself

Rather than sending out e-mails telling people to use the tools, set a different expectation by incorporating the tools that you want your salespeople to use into the conversations you have with them. Here are some examples:

1. Ask to See the Buying Roles Chart for Each Opportunity Your Salesperson Wants You to Get Involved In. Your sales rep might be able to carry around all the names, titles, and organizational relationships for a dozen different people within each of their accounts in their heads. But if you are managing five or six salespeople, you certainly can't. Insist on reviewing a current buying roles chart (Figure 4.3) before you agree to go along on any sales call.

2. Ask to See an Opportunity Scorecard for Each Opportunity Your Salesperson Wants to Strategize About. Unless you have some understanding of why the customer would buy and how they could buy if they wanted to, your advice will naturally be ill-conceived. The opportunity scorecard (Figure 5.1) is an excellent mechanism to drive discussions and establish strategy for each opportunity.

3. Ask to See an Opportunity Review Sheet for Each Client Meeting Your Salesperson Wants to Tell You About. Spending live telephone time or face-to-face time talking about the customer's current state (A) can be a very inefficient use of time. The opportunity review sheet (Figure 6.6) is an excellent way to distribute information about an account to various people on your team who are involved in a particular opportunity. With this information as a foundation, your strategy and opportunity planning sessions will be far more productive.

4. Use the Precall Planning Sheet to Help Create the Agenda for Any Upcoming Client Meeting Your Salesperson Asks You to Attend. Help your salesperson understand that you are not willing to invest your time in an opportunity that is not thoroughly qualified and that you certainly aren't willing to drive or fly to a meeting without a clear plan and well-defined objectives of what you hope to accomplish. Hopefully, they will realize that they shouldn't be willing to either.

*　　*　　*

These are just a few examples of the way your expectations and behavior can drive adoption of the results-based selling tools. If your salesperson shows up to strategize with you without their opportunity review sheet, pull out a blank one and use it to frame the discussion and drive the questions that you ask them. Show them that you value the tools and that you need them in order to do your job well. If you don't use the tools as you interact with your salespeople, they will quickly assume that they simply aren't that important. Leading your salespeople by example requires that *you* use the tools that you want them to use.

Making the Results-Based Selling Method Work for You

This book has been written with one purpose in mind: To help you maximize your selling results. I believe that the best way to do that is make the transition from selling products and services to selling results. This means learning how to help your customers identify and achieve their desired business goals.

To make the results-based selling method work for you, apply the five-step process we talk about at the beginning of this chapter. Figure out where you are now. Decide where you want to go. Develop your plan, and execute that plan. Then measure your results. I encourage you to implement some of these concepts and tools starting today. Pick out one idea or maybe one new tool, and do something with it right now.

Some of the techniques and approaches might feel a little uncomfortable at first. That is to be expected. Anything new takes a little getting used to. But I assure you that over time, if you use them, you will become more comfortable—especially as they begin to produce results for you.

I encourage you to think differently about how you sell. Start to think about the vendor/customer relationship from your customer's point of view. Before you pick up the phone or go see your customer, think about the next logical step in their buying process and what you are going to say or do to help them take that step. Most of all, think about how you can maximize the return on the time you invest in selling. Soon, you'll begin to see measurable improvements in your selling results!

Customer Results Maps

The following diagrams are eight different customer results maps that you can use to develop your business acumen and practice connecting the dots between the functional capabilities of your solutions and some of the desired business results that companies in the industries you sell to might be trying to accomplish. Ideally, you will develop your knowledge of your customers' business models to the point that you could create a unique customer results map for each major customer you work with. You can then use it as a tool to illustrate how your products and services solutions tie to and support the achievement of their specific goals and objectives. These sample customer results maps can act as a starting place.

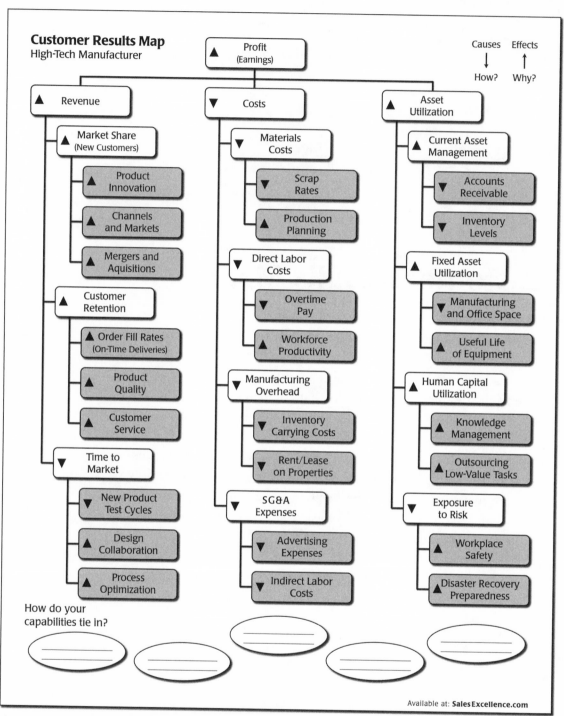

Figure A.1 Customer Results Map—High-Tech Manufacturer

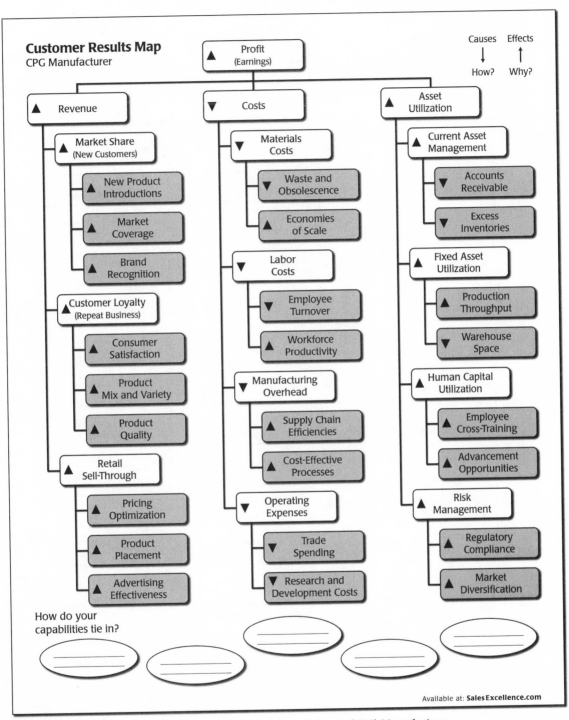

Figure A.2 Customer Results Map—Consumer Packaged Goods (CPG) Manufacturer

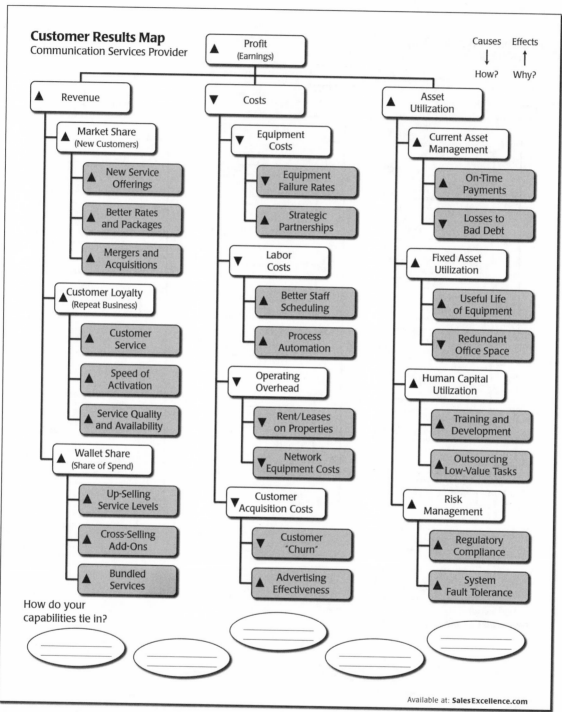

Figure A.3 Customer Results Map—Communication Services Provider

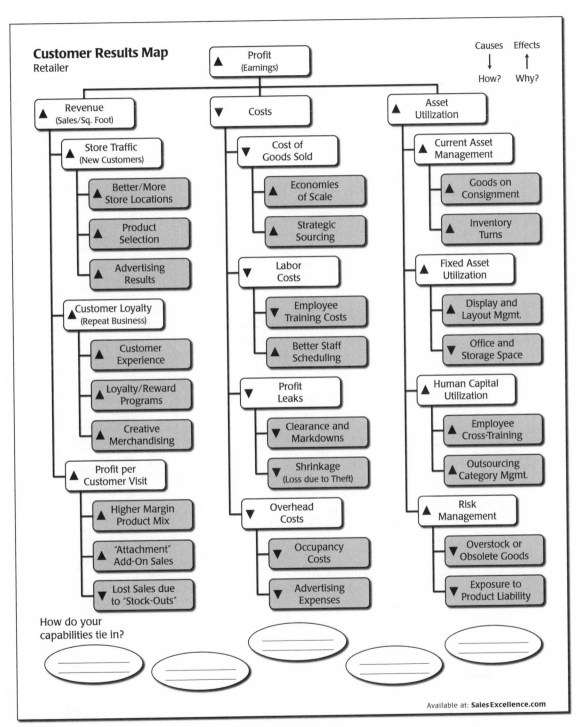

Figure A.4 Customer Results Map–Retailer

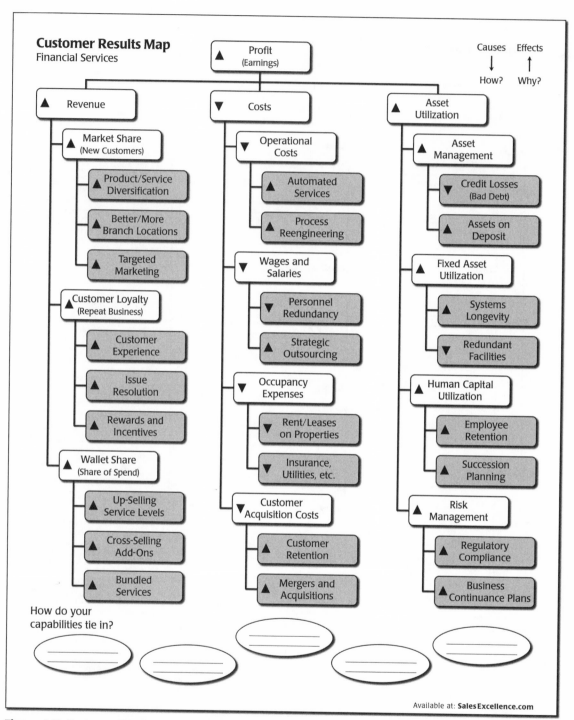

Figure A.5 Customer Results Map—Financial Services

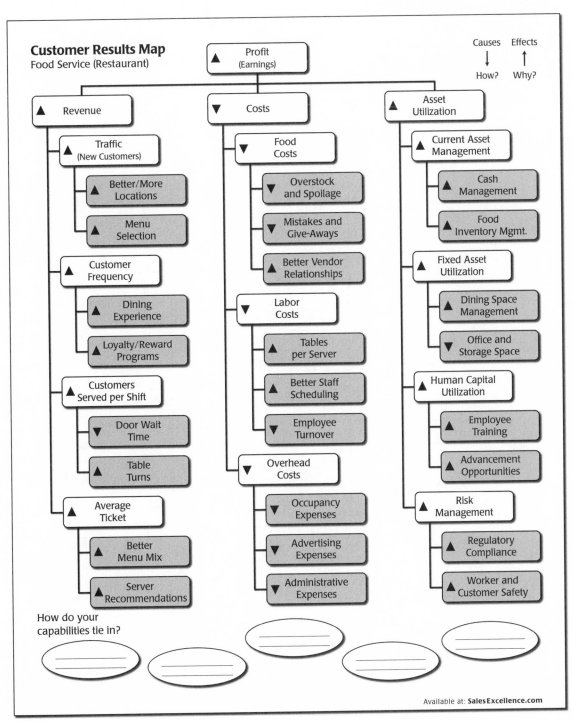

Figure A.6 Customer Results Map—Food Service (Restaurant)

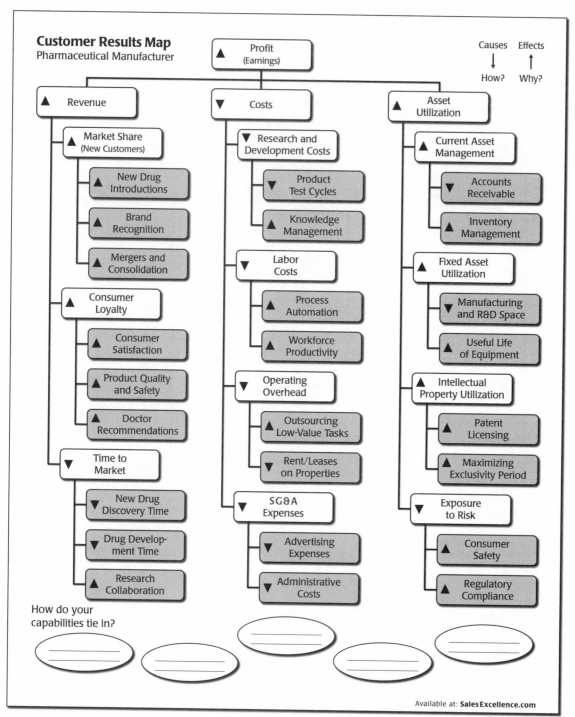

Figure A.7 Customer Results Map–Pharmaceutical Manufacturer

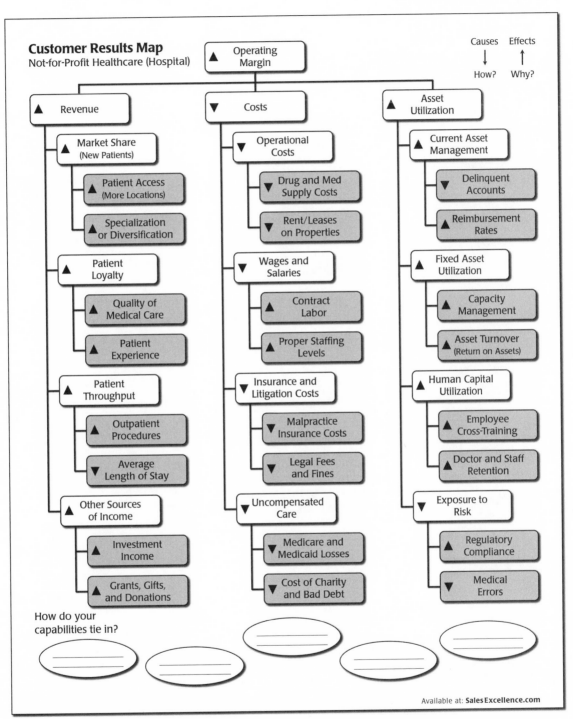

Figure A.8 Customer Results Map—Not-For-Profit Healthcare (Hospital)

Index